GAZA

Wisdom
Editions
Minneapolis

FIRST EDITION 2024
Gaza: Changing the World and Opening Eyes.
Copyright © 2024 by Cathy Sultan. All rights reserved.

10 9 8 7 6 5 4 3 2
ISBN: 978-1-962834-19-3

Cover and interior design: Gary Lindberg

Prase for Cathy Sultan Books

Israeli and Palestinian Voices: A Dialogue with Both Sides
"Standing in the shoes of those who face each other daily across this dangerous divide forces us to see beyond media stereotypes too often reduced to terrorist and victim. The fast-paced narrative and compelling interviews brings to life a conflict whose complexities Americans must try to understand."

–Sarah Harder, President, National Peace Foundation

A Beirut Heart
"There is nothing like an intelligent woman, spouse and mother of small children to carry one into the midst of war, with its horrors as well as its capacity for soul-building. Sultan's narrative enfleshes our disjointed 'news' of the Middle East."

–David Burrell, C.S.C., Hesburgh Professor of Philosophy and Theology, University of Notre Dame; Director, Tantur Ecumenical Institute, Jerusalem

"A view drawn from a camera obscura that moves behind the screen of invading armies, détentes, and broken treaties. A compelling story of survival that settles for no less than the promise that this family will remain together and safe at all cost."

–Colleen McElroy, Professor of English, University of Seattle; author of 14 books including *Over the Lip of the World; Among Storytellers of Madagascar* and *Queen of the Ebony Isles,* which received the American Book Award

Tragedy in South Lebanon

"Tragedy in South Lebanon provides vital information about a topic often misreported by the mainstream media. I particularly liked the interview with both Hezbollah and Israeli soldiers describing the same battle. This is an important book that should be read by anyone interested in Israel and Lebanon."

–Reese Erlich, foreign correspondent and author of
The Iran Agenda: The Real Story of US Policy and the Middle East Crisis

"As anyone who works with other organizations to ban the use, sale and transfer of cluster bombs, I applaud Cathy Sultan's discussion on the effects of these lethal weapons on Lebanese civilians, many of them children, who continue to be killed and maimed by these odious, unexploded Israeli cluster bombs."

–George Cody, PhD, Executive Director, American Task Force for Lebanon

"Finally, finally, finally, there is a book that looks at the many issues Lebanon faces for what they are—complex. We have had enough of the bumper sticker slogans and five second sound bites. Great!"

Jack Rice, ex-CIA officer

"Sultan gives a fair and accurate account of what went on in South Lebanon. As a UN official who has spent 24 years in South Lebanon, I say she also lends a refreshing voice to those who would otherwise never be heard."

-Timor Goksel, Senior Advisor and Official Spokesman for the United Nations Interim Force in Lebanon

GAZA

Changing the World
and Opening Eyes

Cathy Sultan

Wisdom
Editions

Minneapolis

Table of Contents

Also by
Cathy Sultan

A Beirut Heart
Israeli and Palestinian Voices: A
Dialogue with both Sides
Tragedy in South Lebanon
The Syrian
Damascus Street
An Ambassador to Syria
Omar's Choice

October 7, 2023

At approximately 6:30 a.m., on October 7, Hamas fighters stormed communities along Israel's southern fence with Gaza and killed 1,137 people. According to Israeli officials, the dead included 695 civilians, 373 security forces and seventy-one foreign workers. Hamas kidnapped 251 people and took them to Gaza. Israeli authorities have accused Hamas fighters of committing war crimes including torture, rape and mutilation. Hamas has strongly rejected these allegations, particularly those of sexual violence.

By Hamas' actions, Palestinians living in Gaza have incurred the wrath of Israel. As of June 2024, some 37,700 civilians, mostly women and children, have lost their lives with close to 100,000 wounded.

According to the American Jewish Committee, the October 7th Hamas terrorists waged the deadliest attack on Jews since the Nazi "final solution" of the second world war, better known as the Holocaust. They slaughtered babies, raped women, burned whole families alive and took hundreds of innocent civilians hostage.

Al Jazeera's Investigative Unit (1-Unit) carried out a forensic analysis of the events of October 7. It revealed widespread human rights abuses by fighters and others who followed them through the fence from the Gaza Strip. However, 1-Unit's investigation, which examined hours of footage from CCTV, dashcams, personal phones and headcams of killed Hamas fighters, found that many of the stories that circulated after October 7 were false. These included claims of atrocities such as the mass killing and beheading of babies as well as allegations of widespread and systematic rape—stories that were used repeatedly by politicians in Israel and the West to justify the ferocity of the bombardment of the Gaza Strip.

Hillel Schenker, in his article in *The Nation* on October 12, 2023, wrote, "One can perhaps understand Palestinian frustrations, with the expansion of settlements, an Israeli government that declares its goal to be controlling the entire land from the river to the sea with no room for a Palestinian state; provocations on the Temple Mount/Haram al Sharif, the third-holiest site in Islam; settler harassment and threats of another Nakba; a war that could lead to the expulsion of Palestinians from the West Bank. But murdering over 1,000 Israelis, mainly innocent civilians is not a response meant to achieve the basic Palestinian right to freedom, national self-determination and a state of their own."

Introduction

Conflicts rarely produce winners. Palestinians in Gaza continue to fear for their lives while Israelis fare no better with their leaders desperate to remain in power even if it means perpetual war. How difficult would it be to promote peace as an option to open conflict and make it work?

This question prompted me to revisit something I wrote in my memoir *A Beirut Heart* about the possibility of peace in the Middle East. The scene took place in 1976. Civil war was raging in Beirut and my family and I had just escaped on an apple boat to Syria. Upon landing in the seaport town of Lattakia, my husband Michel was unexpectedly arrested. During the interrogation his Syrian guards questioned him not about the supposed charges against him but about Israel. They wanted to know about Israeli technology and what kind of products they made, whether America supplied Israel with its weaponry or if the Israelis manufactured their own. Was it true that Israel had the best hospitals in the Middle East? The mother of one soldier needed open heart surgery. "How wonderful it would be," he said, "if one day we could get into our cars

3

and drive to Israel for treatment."

Three teenage girls I interviewed at their Ramallah high school in the West Bank in 2002 spoke most succinctly about their vision for peace and how it would work. When asked how they would implement it, they responded: "We would forget about Jerusalem, boundaries, the right of return, the generals in the army, and just be one nation. We are all brothers and sisters, all from one family. We feel certain most Israeli children have the same feelings, the same imagination of life as it can and should be."

An Israeli soldier I interviewed on another visit: "I am young and do not want to spend my whole life preparing for war. In Israel we have a war mentality. We never seem to talk about peace. It is as if saying the word is being disloyal to the State of Israel. I am ready to live in peace with my neighbors. I think the Palestinians and Hezbollah in Lebanon want the same. Why aren't our leaders willing to take the leap?"

After living the past forty years in tranquil Eau Claire, Wisconsin, I still reflect on and appreciate how wonderful peace is, when allowed to happen. From time to time I think about dodging snipers and running into shelters, about my apron with its bullet hole, and about rescuing my children from school under a salvo of bombs. I cannot go back to living in such insanity, but I can write about the horrors of war so that our collective national memory can never say, "We didn't know." I can bring to light the voices of ordinary people in Gaza, or Haifa, or the West Bank or the students who protest on college campuses across the United States and beyond, demanding a ceasefire.

Why is this latest explosion seemingly intractable?

What has happened in Israel and in the United States to make this so? This book is an attempt to explain the multiple challenges, not least of which is whether each side has gone beyond any possible notion of reconciliation. As someone who knows intimately both the Israeli and Palestinian positions and who has lived in and frequently visited the region for the last fifty-five years, I take up this challenge.

To my American audience, this conflict is also yours. A basic understanding of the many facets of this festering conflict is vital if it is to end. Knowledge brings power and the power of an informed people, when fully engaged, produces a chain reaction that reaches all the way to the highest levels of power. Our collective voices, when used, limit our leaders' ability to engage in a conflict such as this one that does not threaten our national security or our lives or our livelihood. Excuses for not being better informed vary from willful complacency to being overwhelmed with personal struggles. I get that, and I empathize, but we must start caring what our leaders do in our name. Students across our campuses and beyond understand what is at stake. Despite the threat of sanctions, expulsion and police brutality, they stand, fearless, unified in their demand for a permanent cease fire, and more importantly, they bring issues that could result in a stable Middle East, foremost justice for the Palestinian people. They should not be made to stand alone.

A Brief History of
Student Protests

June 16, 1976, was a major turning point in South African history. It stands as a proud testament to the efficacy of sustained protests in driving social change in the face of one of history's most oppressive systems. The 1976 demonstrations by Soweto school children marked the end of submissiveness by the Black population of South Africa and the beginning of a new form of activism in their struggle against apartheid.

The 1953 Bantu Separation Act enforced a separate, inferior and heavily censored education system. As a result, only 10 percent of blacks had graduated from high school by 1961. The act required Black students to learn Afrikaans to prepare them for manual labor and menial jobs the government deemed suitable for their race. The intent of the act was to instill the idea that Black people should accept being subservient to white South Africa and that the language of instruction was to be Afrikaans, the language of the colonizer. The irony was that most Afrikaners did not speak English, while many Black South Africans spoke it fluently. The attempt to introduce Afrikaans as a language of instruction, supplanting English, was the spark that ignited the Soweto uprising.

For forty-six years, the government of South Africa had enforced racial segregation to maintain a minority white dominance. Blacks were removed from white populated areas and transferred to Black-only townships comprising 13 percent of the land, often with limited resources, while the white settler population claimed the rest. Skilled labor jobs were reserved for White people while labor laws allowed employers to pay blacks significantly less than whites for the same work. Black people could not circulate without a pass and were jailed if they did. The government purged the non-white population from voter rolls, denying them the right to participate in the political processes or have any form of representation. It outlawed interracial marriages and segregated recreational spaces and abolished mixed-race universities.

For the students of South Africa, June 16th,1976 was meant to be the beginning of three days of peaceful demonstrations to protest these government mandates, but the government called out its troops and over a two-day period killed 150 students. Over the next six months, when the protests continued, the government killed 600 more students. Unable to silence them, the government went after the leaders of not only the African National Congress, exiling some and imprisoning others for life, like Nelson Mandela, they went after Steve Biko, the leader of the South African Students' Organization. They arrested him under the terrorism act and bludgeoned him to death on September 12, 1977.

If the Soweto Uprising catalyzed student protests, the death of Steve Biko galvanized international outrage. That momentum pressured western universities to divest from apartheid-related investments in South Africa. Ultimately, economic pressure led to comprehensive sanctions by the US and the UK neither of which could ignore their own complicity in the apartheid regime. That was the final blow for the government of South Africa. In 1989 President Frederik de Klerk unbanded the African National Congress, released Nelson Mandela from prison and negotiated a transition to majority rule across South Africa. In 1993 Mandela's coalition won the first all-inclusive election. Four years later he was sworn in as South Africa's first Black president, yet it took the US government until July 1, 2008, fifteen years after he became president, to remove him from their terrorist list.

Not unlike the South Africans, the Palestinians face similar challenges. The Israeli government, at least until recently, managed to make their military occupation and coercion tactics against the Palestinian people invisible to the outside world. Jeff Halper, Coordinator of the Israeli Committee against House Demolitions, called Israel's repressive system the "The Matrix of Control." Expropriation of Palestinian land to construct Israeli settlements; Israeli control of 90 percent of former Palestine; a massive system of highways for Israeli-use only; control over all aquifers; work discrimination; travel permits restricting movement; displacement through exile; house demolitions; a freeze on development and restrictions on the planting of crops and their sale;

collective punishment; settler violence and assassinations, overseen by Israeli soldiers, of activists and political leaders. In all, there are at least sixty-five Israeli laws that discriminate against Palestinian citizens of Israel. One of them, passed in 2018, declared the country a "nation state of the Jewish people." This new law formally endorsed the use of apartheid methods within Israel's recognized borders. On January 26, 2024, the International Court of Justice found plausible evidence of Israel committing genocide against Palestinians.

Students across US college campuses are protesting the injustice they see perpetrated against the Palestinian people and demand their government take actions to stop these atrocities. Like the students in Soweto, US students face a government whose structures persist in perpetuating Israel's grave abuses. They fear such protests will spread and disrupt their long established status quo and respond by calling in the police and the national guard to quelch the peaceful protests. The students refuse to be deterred. This is their chosen battleground where they hope to see a formidable Israeli government defanged and the Palestinian people liberated.

Historically, students have faced stiff challenges. During the Civil Rights Movement, the Nonviolent Coordinating Committee comprised mostly of Black college students played a vital role in the Civil Rights Movement through their nonviolent protests and sit-ins and like the students today, were assaulted for their bravery. Through their steadfastness, the movement broke the pattern of segregation by "race" in the south, which led to equal rights legislation for African Americans and greater social and economic mobility.

The anti-Viet Nam protests across college campuses during the late 60s, early 70s played a significant role in shaping public opinion and ultimately contributed to the withdrawal of US troops from Viet Nam. This movement was one of the most pervasive displays of opposition to government policy in modern times.

If there is a difference between previous protests and current ones playing out on college campuses, it is that today students have taken up a cause not for their own rights but for the rights of others at the expense of their safety, their reputation and livelihoods. Their actions are nothing less than noble.

The comparison between South Africa and Israel reveals stark similarities, yet the oppressive measures employed by the Israeli state on Palestinians, to the admission of South Africans themselves, has surpassed those measures undertaken by their government. As survivors of apartheid, Black South Africans are uniquely qualified to identify apartheid for as Nelson Mandela said, "We know too well that our freedom is not complete without that of the Palestinian people." How fitting it is then that it was the South African government that brought the charge of genocide against the apartheid State of Israel asserting that Palestinians have endured a violent military occupation that has deprived them of their historical rights. They further charged that Gaza has suffered a seventeen-year military blockade by air, sea and air, and has undergone a live-streamed genocide since October 7, 2023. The Global South supports this charge. The fight now is in the Global North where the Israeli government relies on the full and unconditional support of the White House and both houses of Congress,

11

regardless of which party is in power, to whitewash their crimes. These are the same centers of power that backed South Africa's apartheid government and branded figures like Nelson Mandela, a man who left a legacy of peace, reconciliation and social justice, a terrorist.

There are endless videos showing confrontations between demonstrators, whether Arab Americans or Jews, and police on college campuses, standing up against the genocide in Gaza. But these students are much more. They represent humanity and it is their passion, their resilience and unwavering support for justice that will change the conversation. Their actions are the glue that holds our fragile world together and yet they are beaten and arrested for their actions because they dare challenge the legitimacy of our leaders and their abuse of power. Viewed in this light, it is easy to see what the Israeli genocide is doing beyond the unconscionable suffering in Gaza. It is difficult to overstate the significance of this moment. Those exercising power have opened the gates to a dangerous new level of suppression of free speech, free association and open dissent, and a twisted perversion of public discourse. Palestinians have no place in Israel's story. When they stand and fight for their freedom, they are labeled terrorists and treated as threats to the country's security while individuals defending Palestinian's right to self-determination are accused of antisemitism, charges that have become ubiquitous because they are useful to those who discredit the truth, the same truth students defend with their lives.

Whether it is the vilification of students from members of Congress or their calls for punishment, these are troubling times. As Michael Brenner said in his May 23rd article "A Brutal Suppression of Speech" in Consortium News, "There is an absence of overt, tangible national interest at stake. This is not Viet Nam that could be rationalized in terms of the Cold War because nothing currently happening in Palestine/Israel poses a threat to the security of the US. There is no cherished principle that US leaders feel obligated to uphold; quite the opposite, the US itself is an accomplice to gross crimes against humanity."

Brenner pointed out that, "The protests were peaceful with no damage to property. The couple of exceptions that involved breakups prompted the authorities to quickly resort to severe penalties. Overall, students have been acting in accordance with the vaunted principles of freedom of speech and freedom of assembly in a cause of humanistic concern for others, free of self-interest."

One telling incident of violence occurred at UCLA when a masked gang of pro-Israeli supporters armed with clubs and teargas assaulted an encampment of peaceful students under cover of night. Fifteen of the victims were hospitalized. The attack continued for three hours under the watchful eye of the LAPD who refused to intervene. To date, only one of the assailants has been arrested.

Charges of antisemitism are now commonplace because they are useful to those who wish to discredit the students. The US House of Representatives recently passed legislation defining antisemitism in terms so broad that criticism of Israel will, if the Senate passes the bill, be considered antisemitic. It is otherwise difficult to overstate the significance of this moment. As Patrick Lawrence said in his May 10 article *"The Truth of our Time,"* "those exercising power have opened the door to a dangerous new level of repression—suppression of free speech, free association and open dissent, the grotesque perversion of public discourse its most malign feature. This is our new reality. A full-dress attack on the truth."

When students began protesting, many political, corporate and media figures committed themselves to the reality Israel has created and are determined to see it continue. A Washington Post investigation dated May 16 revealed that a group of billionaires and business leaders had secretly formed a chat group shortly after October 7 with the goal of creating a narrative favorable to Israel. It read: "While Israel works to win the physical war, the chat group's members should help win the war of US public opinion by funding an information campaign against Hamas." Their activities reached into the highest levels of the Israeli government, the US business community and elite universities. Their message offered a view into how they planned to use their money, influence and power to make genocide appear acceptable. President Biden's recent remarks implicitly sent the same message: Dissent if you wish, but we will pay no attention. In the case of Gaza, there is our version of events, and there is no place for any other.

The Guardian, in a piece dated May 7, referenced a letter signed by 750 Jewish students that went largely unreported in the US. It read in part, "As Jewish students, we wholeheartedly reject the narrative that the Gaza solidarity encampments are inherently antisemitic. This narrative is part of a decades-long effort to blur the lines between criticism of Israel and antisemitism. It is a narrative that ignores the large populations of Jewish students participating in and helping to lead the encampments as a true expression of their Jewish values."

The Gaza Strip

The Gaza Strip, an area one-eighth the size of Rhode Island, represents 1 percent of historic Palestine. The Strip is approximately twenty-five miles long and seven miles wide and is home to 2.3 million Palestinians. The Strip is one of two Palestinian territories, the other being the West Bank. On the eastern coast of the Mediterranean Sea, Gaza is bordered by Egypt to the south and Israel to the north and east. It has been sealed off by air, land and sea by the Government of Israel since 2005. The inhabitants are descendants of those who fled Palestine or were expelled by Israeli forces in 1948 when Israel declared itself a state. In 1967, during the Israeli-Arab war, Israel captured and occupied the Gaza Strip, East Jerusalem, the West Bank and Syria's Golan Heights, initiating decades of occupation of Palestinian territories. On July 15, 1967, only five weeks after the end of the war, Israel quietly established its first settlements in the occupied territories, despite promises to Washington that it would not do so. Fifty-seven years later, there are 800,000 settlers living illegally in the West Bank; in East

15

Jerusalem there are fourteen settlements housing 230,000. In the Golan Heights there are thirty settlements, home to an estimated 20,000 people. Based on numerous U.N. resolutions that cite Article 49 of the Geneva Convention, all Israeli settlements are illegal and constitute a violation of international law. In December 1967, U.N. Resolution 242 was unanimously passed by the Security Council requiring the establishment of a just and lasting peace in the Middle East, which included the withdrawal of Israeli armed forces from all occupied territories.

In the mid-1990s the Oslo Accords established the Palestinian Authority (PA) as a limited governing authority, initially led by the secular party Fatah until that party's electoral defeat in 2006 to Hamas when it took over governance of Gaza. In 2005, Israel unilaterally withdrew its military forces from Gaza, dismantled its settlements and implemented a military blockade and occupation which prevents people and goods from freely entering or leaving the territory, making it an open-air prison, controlled air, sea and land by Israel. The closure since the start of the conflict has contributed to the deaths of tens of thousands of Palestinian, primarily women and children, and an ongoing famine.

More than 70 percent of Gaza's population are refugees or descendants of refugees, half of whom are under the age of eighteen. Sunni Muslims make up most of the Gazan population with a Palestinian Christian minority. Gaza's unemployment rate is among the highest in the world, with an overall unemployment rate of 46 percent and a youth unemployment rate of 70 percent. Despite this, Gaza's literacy rate is 88 percent while youth literacy rate is 97 percent.

On November 29, 1974, U.N. General Assembly resolution 3,246 affirmed "the legitimacy of a people's struggle for liberation from colonial and foreign domination by all means including armed struggle to protect itself." Otherwise stated, a people under colonial domination, i.e., the Palestinians, have the right to use armed struggle against their aggressor, Isael, and its military and police forces.

Divestment, Another Student Demand

Students are calling for their universities to disclose and divest from companies linked to Israel and its war in Gaza. What does this mean? Divestment is a process through which an organization sells off its shares, assets or other investments for political, ethical or financial reasons, according to the Cornell Law School website. In the case of a university, to divest would mean to pull out of investments in certain companies made with money from the university's endowment fund. Universities rely on endowments to fund things like research and scholarships, and those endowments are typically invested in companies and alternative asset classes, such as private equity and hedge funds. Calls for divestment are not new in the movement against Israeli occupation of Palestine.

They are central to the Boycott, Divestment and Sanctions (BDS) movement, an international effort calling for the boycott of companies accused of being complicit in the occupation of the Palestinian territory, the war in

Gaza and violating international law. To date, BDS has claimed many successes. That list can be found on the US Campaign for Palestinian Rights website.

The protesters at Columbia University call for Columbia to divest from corporations that they believe profit from Israel's war in Gaza. They listed the names of some of these companies in a leaflet passed around during the campus encampments. They Include, among others, Lockheed Martin, HEICO, BlackRock, Google and Microsoft. The New York University alumni for Palestine website calls on NYU to "terminate all vendor contracts with companies playing active roles in the military occupation in Palestine and ongoing genocide in Gaza, namely Cisco, Lockheed Martin, Caterpillar and General Electric. Equipment made by Caterpillar was gifted to Israel through the same program."

Students at other campuses are calling for greater transparency regarding their institutions' investments. Cisco, for example, revealed that it had established a long-term partnership with Israel in 2018 to develop government-subsidized co-working hubs to help integrate small towns and remote regions to the Israeli high-tech industry. Some of these hubs were in the Occupied Palestinian Territory and Syria's Golan Heights.

Maryland-headquartered Lockheed Martin is the world's largest military company and supplies Israel with weapons that are gifted to Israel through the US government's Foreign Military Financing program. Equipment made by US bulldozer manufacturer Caterpillar was gifted Israel through the same financing program. The Israeli military uses Caterpillar D9 bulldozers to demolish Palestinian properties. Engines and electric power and mechanical systems of Boston-based General Electric are integrated into the Israeli military's fighter jets, attack helicopters and surveillance aircraft.

Christopher Marsicano, an assistant professor of educational studies at Davidson College in North Carolin, who researched the impact of divestment from fossil fuels on university endowments, a demand from previous student protests, said, "Divestment is hard to do but the political impact of the demand is significant. The student protests have captured the attention of the Israeli government and are putting some pressure on stakeholders to support a ceasefire. However, it would be difficult for most universities managing large endowment funds to divest from all the companies that do business with Israeli and weapons manufacturers. Marsicano explained that university endowment fund managers at most US colleges are "doing what most Americans who have a retirement fund are doing. They are investing in index funds and private equity. Index funds offer investors exposure to all the companies listed on one specific index of shares. A fund tracking FTSE 100, for example, holds shares in all 100 of the largest companies listed on London Stock Exchange. Investors in the tracker fund cannot pick and choose which shares to hold. Tracker funds are a popular form of investment for large institutional pension or endowment funds because they provide a safe way to diversify holdings thereby reducing risk. As companies' share prices rise and fall, so do their market capitalizations, the value of all their stocks, which means companies can drop in and out of different indices, making it tricky for investors to screen out specific companies.

Resistance to the protesters demands is strong because many universities do not want to disclose their financial entanglement, so they claim divestment is impossible. However, the powerful influence of previous divestment movements contributed to transformative systemic change in global politics, specifically the fall of apartheid in South Africa. Students will continue to stand by their demand of divestment and transparency.

Genocide, Zionism, Apartheid and Antisemitism

The definition of **GENOCIDE** in the Convention on the Prevention and Punishment of the Crime of Genocide includes deliberately inflicting on a group conditions of life that are calculated to bring about its physical destruction in whole or in part. Under the current version of the Geneva Convention, the term genocide, more fully means any of the following acts committed with intent to destroy, in whole or in part, a national, ethnical, racial or religious group, such as killing members of the group; causing serious bodily or mental harm to members of the group; deliberately inflicting on the group conditions of life calculated to bring about its physical destruction in whole or in part; imposing measures intended to prevent births within the group; forcibly transferring children of the group to another group. The convention does not say that all five of these acts must be met. It says, "any" of them committed "with intent to destroy, in whole or in part, a national, ethnical, racial or religious group."

In its order published on January 26, 2024, the International Court of Justice (ICJ) found "plausible" evidence of Israel committing genocide against Palestinians. In March, the U.N. Special Rapporteur on the Situation of Human Rights in the Occupied Palestinian Territory, Francesca Albanese, published a monumental report called "Anatomy of a Genocide." In it, Albanese wrote that "there are reasonable grounds to believe that the threshold indicating Israel's commission of genocide is met. More broadly, they also indicate that Israel's actions have been driven by a genocidal logic integral to its settler-colonial project in Palestine, signaling a tragedy foretold."

Intent to commit genocide is easily proven in the context of Israel's bombardment. In October 2023, Israel's President Isaac Herzog said that "an entire nation out there is responsible for the attacks on October 7, and it was not true that "civilians were not aware, not involved." The ICJ pointed to this statement, among many others, because it expressed Israel's intent and use of collective punishment, a genocidal war crime. In November, Israel's Jerusalem Affairs and Heritage Minister, Amichai Eliyahu, said that "dropping a nuclear bomb on Gaza was an option since there are no no-combatants in Gaza." Before the ICJ ruling was published, Moshe Saada, a member of the Israeli Parliament from Netanyahu's Likud Party, said that "all Gazans must be destroyed." These sentiments, by any international standard, demonstrate an intent to commit genocide. As with "apartheid" and "occupation," the use of the term "genocide" is entirely accurate.

ZIONISM is a 19th Century political ideology that claims Jewish safety requires a Jewish-only nation state. The Zionist movement emphasized its ideology as a response to centuries of antisemitic persecution against Jews across Europe. Six years ago, the Israeli Knesset passed the Jewish nation state law codifying that "the right to exercise national self-determination in the State of Israel is unique to the Jewish people."

APARTHEID: The Israeli government treats the Palestinian minority population (21 percent) within its borders as second-class citizens. There are at least sixty-five Israeli laws that discriminate against Palestinian citizens of Israel. One of them, passed in 2018, declared the country "a nation state of the Jewish people." As the Israeli philosopher Omri Boehm wrote, "Through the new law passed in 2018 that declares Israel the nation state of the Jewish people, the Israeli government formally endorses the use of apartheid methods within Israel's recognized borders." The United Nations, Human Rights Watch, Amnesty International and Israel's own human rights group B'Tselem have all stated that Israel's treatment of the Palestinians falls under the definition of apartheid.

ANTISEMITISM, according to the International Holocaust Remembrance Alliance (IHRA), is a certain perception of Jews, which may be expressed as hatred toward Jews. Rhetorical and physical manifestations of antisemitism are directed toward Jewish individuals and or their property, toward Jewish community institutions and religious facilities. This working definition and legally non-binding version was adopted in 2016 by the US State Department. It is used by the US Commission on Civil Rights to help universities identify the lines between hatred and non-hateful incidents.

Equating Antizionism
with Antisemitism

The US House of Representatives voted in May 2024 to approve the Antisemitism Awareness Act. If approved by the Senate, this bill would codify the criminalization of anti-Israeli sentiments by equating antizionism with antisemitism. It would codify a definition of antisemitism established by the International Holocaust Remembrance Alliance (IHRA) which defines anti-semitism as "a certain perception of Jews, which may be expressed as hatred toward Jews." The IHRA definition of antisemitism also includes the targeting of the State of Israel, conceived as a Jewish collectivity. As written, this bill could potentially be used to bar funding of any institution perceived to be advocating support for the Palestinian cause. It would also likely chill free speech by both students and faculty on college campuses by incorrectly equating criticism of the Israeli government with antisemitism which is already protected in the IHRA language. It will most certainly contradict the core mission of universities and all institutions of learning which is to encourage debate, foster dissent and prepare the future leaders of our society to tolerate even profound differences of opinions. It is why it is more urgent than ever to collectively resist the temptation to silence students and faculty members because the halls of power and beyond deem their views offensive to their political ideology or agenda. This is just one hurdle students on campuses face across the US. However, false claims of antisemitism are not new.

In January 2023, Philip Weiss, Founder and Editor-in-Chief of *Mondoweiss*, wrote that, "Kenneth Roth, former Director of Human Rights Watch, which had labeled Israel an apartheid state, was attacked because he said that antisemitism in the West is engendered by Israel's human rights abuses. "Antisemitism is always wrong," Roth said, "and it long preceded the creation of Israel, but the surge of antisemitic incidents during the recent Gaza conflict gives the lie to those who pretend that the Israeli government's conduct doesn't affect antisemitism."

Roth elaborated on this on January 19, 2024, when he spoke to Americans for Peace Now. "I personally have been lambasted when I've noted that incidents of antisemitism sometimes parallel the Israeli government's conduct. With the latest bombardment of Gaza, there is predictably a surge of antisemitism around the world. And to point that out is a taboo. You're never allowed to suggest that the Israeli government, which is supposed to be the custodian of the Jewish People, the savior of the Jewish people, can ever be harming the Jewish people. The Anti-Defamation League, however, charges that critics of Israel who report on Israeli government violations, are the ones fueling antisemitism. So they want it both ways," said Roth.

Reverend Bruce Shipman, Professor at Yale University, wrote in the *New York Times* during the Gaza massacre of 2014 that, "when there are reports of an antisemitism spike the best antidote to antisemitism would be for Israel's patrons abroad to press the Israeli government to give Palestinians freedom." Shipman lost his job at Yale for uttering those words.

The sociologist and liberal Zionist Nathan Glazer issued a similar warning in 1976 about Jewish political support when Israel's illegal occupation of the Palestinian territories was new and expanding. He wrote that "American Jews have become the political prop for Israel in a world that is becoming critical of its actions and Americans could become hostile to Jews as a result." He also warned Jews of the dangers of lobbying for Israel. "American Jews unabashedly lobby for pro-Israel measures with Congress and make it politically uncomfortable to be against Israel. The political figure who does will be subject to much pressure and name-calling, some of it quite unfair."

The British Jewish Middle East expert Tony Klug warned in an address to J Street in 2015 that Israel's dependence on American Jews to defend the indefensible would contribute to an upsurge in antisemitism. "I fear that Israel's never-ending occupation of the land and lives of another people is not just seriously endangering Israel, not to mention deepening the despair of the Palestinians, but it is also making the situation of the Jews around the world increasingly precarious."

Antisemitism is fueled by pro-Israel groups like the American-Israel Political Action Committee (AIPAC) who hold sway over members of Congress. AIPAC openly boasts it plans to spend hundreds of millions of dollars to unseat any member of Congress who is supportive of Palestinian rights and critical of Israel in the 2024 election.

However, there is a new player on the block. In March, Jewish Voice for Peace (JVP) joined a coalition of twenty different progressive organizations to protect pro-Palestinian lawmakers and take on AIPAC. The coalition which calls itself Reject AIPAC has promised to launch a seven-figure electoral defense campaign for lawmakers who have been targeted by AIPAC for their criticism of Israel. In November 2023, Columbia University suspended JVP's student chapter alongside Students for Justice in Palestine after mass student protests erupted on campus against the ongoing Israeli war on Gaza. The suspension led to widespread outrage among students and faculty who called on the university to reinstate both groups. Both JVP and IfNotNow have never denied the October 7 violence by Hamas. They have simply called for a ceasefire and have used the word genocide to describe Israeli attacks on Gaza, and the word apartheid to describe the causes of October 7. The organized Jewish community has ostracized these two groups because it demands Jewish unanimity. Is there an upsurge in antisemitism as the organized Jewish community claims or is it rage at American Jewish organizations for their blind support of Israel?

The biggest promoter of antisemitism is Israeli Prime Minister Netanyahu. According to him the outrageous decision by the International Criminal Court

(ICC) on May 20, 2024, to seek arrest warrants against the democratically elected leaders of Israel, is a moral outrage of historic proportions. He further claims this decision will cast an everlasting mark of shame on the international court. "Israel is waging a just war against Hamas, a genocidal terrorist organization that perpetrated the worst attack on the Jewish people since the Holocaust. Hamas massacred 1,200 Jews, raped Jewish women, burned Jewish babies and took hundreds of hostages. What a travesty of justice. The prosecutor's absurd charges against me and Israel's defense minister are merely an attempt to deny Israel the basic right of self-defense. To all the enemies of Israel, including their collaborators in The Hague, I renew my pledge. Israel will wage its war against Hamas until that war is won."

Israeli scholar David Shulman recently wrote: "The wave of anti-Israeli feelings that is engulfing large numbers of people in the western world has emerged not merely from the Gaza war, but because of the unbearable civilian casualties and mass starvation. What that wave reflects, more profoundly, is the justified disgust with the ongoing occupation, its seemingly eternal and ever more brutal continuation and the policies of massive theft and apartheid that are its very essence. The essential fight against antisemitism cannot mean ongoing degradation and suppression of another people, nor can it be waging a war until it is won, as Mr. Netanyahu suggests."

Police Brutality and Scare Tactics

Police brutality is not new to protest movements but this time the violent crackdown on students on the Columbia University campus involve a new player, a member of the school's own faculty. According to Max Blumenthal, Editor-in-Chief of *The Grayzone*, Adjunct Columbia professor Rebecca Weiner also moonlighted as the head of the New York Police Department's counterterrorism bureau and the person who monitored the situation on campus. She is the granddaughter of Stanislaw Ulam, the Polish Jewish mathematician who helped conceive the hydrogen bomb as part of the Manhattan Project. She maintained an office at Columbia's School of International and Public Affairs (SIPA) Her bio describes her as an Adjunct Associate Professor of International and Public Affairs. She simultaneously serves as the civilian executive in charge of the New York City Police Department's Intelligence and Counterterrorism Bureau. This bureau currently maintains an office in Tel Aviv where it coordinates with Israel's security apparatus and maintains a department liaison.

The image of the once-friendly cop on the beat has been replaced by intimidating, fully armed military-style troops. Israel has played a part in this transition. At least 300 high ranking sheriffs and police from agencies large and small, from New York to Orange County to Ferguson, Missouri, have traveled to Israel for privately funded seminars in what is described as counterterrorism techniques. Since 2002, the Anti-Defamation League (ADL), the American Jewish Committee's Project Interchange and the Jewish Institute for National Security Affairs have sent policy heads, assistant chiefs and captains on fully paid trips to Israel and the Palestinian Occupied Territories to observe the operations of the Israeli security police, the Israeli Defense Forces (IDF), the Israeli border patrol and the country's intelligence agencies.

As far back as 2011 an Associated Press investigation revealed that a "Demographic Unit" operated secretly within the NYPD's Counterterrorism and Intelligence Bureau. This unit spied on Muslims around the New York City area, on Muslim students at Yale and Rutgers in New Jersey, who were involved in Palestinian solidarity activism. This unit was developed in tandem with the CIA and appears to have been inspired by Israeli intelligence as well. During the NYPD's post-raid press conference on the Columbia University encampment, Weiner blamed outsider agitators for triggering the military-style police crackdown. According to her, the police response was not necessitated by any criminal behavior, but by the radical language and symbols of the students. "This was not about students expressing ideas," she claimed. "The real problem was the alleged change in tactics by protesters, which she said represented a "normalization and mainstreaming of rhetoric associated with terrorism." Proof of this dynamic was in what she claimed was the common trend of wearing of headbands associated with foreign terrorist organizations on college campuses.

Mayor Eric Adams, on the other hand, cast the crackdown on student speech as the only possible solution to ongoing campus encampments, citing undefined threats to the minds of impressionable youth. "Young people are being influenced by those who are professionals at radicalizing our children," without specifying anyone in particular, "and I'm not going to allow that to happen as mayor of the city of New York."

Mayor Adams is also no stranger to influence by powerful forces. According to a May 16 article in The *Washington Post,* a group of Jewish billionaires and business executives who launched a $50 million public relations campaign to promote Israel's narrative of the October 7th attack played a significant role in police suppression by privately pressing the New York mayor to send the police to disperse pro-Palestinian protests at Columbia University. According to private WhatsApp messages obtained by the *Post,* and people familiar with the group, Jewish business executives, including Kind snack company founder Daniel Lubetzky, hedge fund manager Daniel Loeb, billionaire Len Blavatnik, and real estate investor Joseph Sitt, organized the call on April 26 with Mayor Adams to encourage him to send police to suppress student protests at Columbia University opposing Israel's ongoing genocide in Gaza. Other group members included former Starbucks CEO Howard Schultz, Dell founder and CEO Michael Dell, hedge fund manager Bill Ackman and Joshua

Kushner, founder of Thrive Capital and brother of Jared Kushner. A log of chat messages showed that during the conference call, some attendees promised political donations to Adams's re-election campaign while others offered to pay for private investigators to assist New York police in targeting protesters. The chat log shows Adams accepted the offer.

The group eventually included about 100 members, more than a dozen of whom are on *Forbes's* annual list of billionaires. The *Post* added: "Overall, the messages offered a window into how many prominent individuals have wielded their money and power to shape American views on the Gaza war, as well as the actions of academics, business and political leaders, including Mayor Adams. Members of the group worked with the Israeli government to screen a roughly 40-minute propaganda film showing footage compiled by the Israeli army, Michael Herzog, the Israeli ambassador to the US, war cabinet member Benny Ganz and former prime minister Naftali Bennett to audiences in New York City. The film sought to promote false claims attributed to Hamas in its horrific attack on October 7. The group's mission? While Israel worked to win the physical war, the chat group's members would help win the war of US public opinion by funding an information campaign. The news site *Semafor* reported in November 2023 that Sternlicht, CEO of Starwood Capital Group, launched a $50 million anti-Hamas media campaigns with various Wall Street and Hollywood billionaires. He promised that all contributions to the media campaign would remain anonymous. "I'm sensitive to concerns about being less effective if it appears that this is a Jewish initiative."

Bill Ackman in an October 10th tweet wrote, "I have been asked by a number of CEOs if Harvard would release a list of the members of each of the Harvard organizations that issued a letter assigning sole responsibility for Hamas' heinous acts to Israel so as to insure none of us inadvertently hire any of their members."

Billionaire investor Kenneth Griffin called on his alma mater Harvard to embrace "Western values," saying that the turmoil across college campuses was the product of a "Cultural Revolution" in US education. In an interview with the *Financial Times* he said that the US has "lost sight of education as a means of pursuing truth and acquiring knowledge. Harvard should put front and center that it stands for meritocracy in America."

CEO Leon Cooperman had hard words for Ivy League students who are sharing anti-Israel sentiments on campus. He told The Claman Countdown host, Liz Clamen, that "These kids at these colleges have shit for brains. We have one reliable ally in the Middle East. That's Israel. We only have one democracy in the Middle East. That's Israel. And we have one economy tolerant of different people—gays, lesbians, etc. That's Israel. So these young kids have no idea what they're doing. Now the real shame is I've given Columbia probably around $50 million over many years. Now I'm going to suspend my giving. I'll give to other organizations."

Funding attacks on the pro-Palestinian student movements were not limited to the East Coast. At UCLA, counter protesters conducted several rounds of attacks against the Gaza solidarity encampment by releasing bags of mice injected with an unknown substance, and cockroaches. They tormented students with constant loud noises including air raid sirens, racial epithets and sounds of a baby wailing. When called, police took hours to arrive, and when they did, not a single counter demonstrator was arrested. For the Zionist counterpoint at UCLA a GoFundMe for the counterdemonstrators was established. It raised $97,000. Among its donors was Jessica Seinfeld, the wife of prominent comedian Jerry Seinfeld. She gave $5,000.

According to James Bamford in his December 22, 2023 article in *The Nation,* "Canary Mission is a massive blacklisting and doxing operation directed from Israel that targets students and professors critical of Israeli policies, and then launches slanderous charges against them, charges designed to embarrass and humiliate them and damage their future employability, all secretly funded by wealthy Jewish Americans and Jewish American foundations."

Like its campus spy operation, Israel on Campus Coalition, Canary Mission acts as a key intelligence asset for the Ministry of Strategic Affairs, a highly secretive intelligence organization that is largely focused on the US and on Israel's Shin Bet security service. Any Jewish or Palestinian activist on their list will likely find themselves detained and questioned or denied permission if they attempt to enter Israel. Canary Mission agents have also been involved in physical intimidation. At George Washington University in 2018, on the eve of a vote on a student-government resolution calling for divestment from companies profiting from Israeli violations of Palestinian human rights, two powerful men in yellow canary outfits suddenly turned up in the lobby of the building in which the vote was to take place. They proceeded to engage in a strange and frightening dance, the purpose of which was to warn students against the resolution, while hackling them with a chilling chant, "There are no secrets. We'll know how you vote, and we'll act accordingly."

Again, James Bamford, "Rather than drag university presidents up to Capitol Hill for a replay of the Red Scare/HUAC hearings, it's time for the White House and Congress, now and in any future administration, to at last rip the cover off Israel's vast network of spies, collaborators and funders in this country, even if it means giving up millions of donations and political support from AIPAC, the key reason Israel remains immune from any investigation."

* * *

To the billionaires and the Israeli agencies running Canary Mission and to the president and members of Congress, who want to silence and intimidate university students, we, the university students, offer multiple responses.

"President Biden, we urge you to resist the temptation to silence students and faculty members because powerful voices deem our views offensive. Instead, we urge you to defend the universities' core mission of encouraging debate, fostering dissent and preparing the future leaders of our pluralistic society to tolerate even profound differences of opinion. We will win this battle, Mr. President, because our solidarity is stronger than those who seek to divide and pit us against one another. Our work is just beginning. Eight months into the Israeli government's genocide, we are still fighting for a permanent ceasefire, and we will continue to do so because we are the conscience of a nation."

"We're not just responding to Israeli apartheid and genocide, we're trying to build our own vision of a society where you see people doing Qu'ran recitations, and reading Sabbat services on the same encampment tarp, that's the kind of world we want to build."

"We're perceived as a threat, causing people to feel unsafe. We're portrayed as being violent when it's the universities who are calling in police, clad in riot gear, who use pepper spray, rubber bullets, stun grenades and teargas, to arrest a thousand of us. We're simply drawing on traditions, fundamental to American political culture, of sit-ins, hunger strikes and peaceful encampments. The strikes date to pre-colonial struggles before that, to India, to Ireland, to the struggle against apartheid in South Africa. Palestine is just the most obvious example in the world today. The struggle against Israeli occupation is viewed accurately by Zionists both within the US and Israel, as the last dying gasp of imperialism. They're scared it will disappear. The liberation of Palestine would mean a radically different world, a world that moves past exploitation and injustice. Imagine how wonderful that would be. That's why so many people who are not Palestinian, who are not Arab or Muslim, are so invested in this struggle. They see its significance."

"Mr. President, if someone speaks more about violent encampments than they do about violent genocide of the Palestinians, they have a problem reflective of deep and dangerous biases."

Genocide

The term "genocide" was coined for the specific purpose of naming the systematic, state-sponsored persecution of the Jewish people during the Holocaust. Recognition of the special nature of Jewish suffering has given way to frequent accusations, rightly or wrongly, that Jews seek to benefit from an exclusive claim of victimhood, that they have weaponized the Holocaust to insulate Israel from all criticism and moral obligation. The manipulation of the Holocaust and the concept of genocide is textbook antisemitism, according to the widely adopted International Holocaust Remembrance Alliance's definition. The assault on Gaza is a textbook case of genocide.

On January 26, 2024, the International Court of Justice found that there was plausible evidence that Israel has committed acts that violate the Genocide Convention. In a provisional order delivered by the court's president, Joan O'Donoghue, the court said Israel must ensure "with immediate effect" that its forces not commit any of the acts prohibited by the convention. O'Donoghue said the court cannot make a final decision right now on whether

Israel is guilty of genocide, but she said, given the deteriorating situation in Gaza, the court has jurisdiction to order measures to protect Gaza's population from further risk of genocide. By sixteen votes to 1, the court voted that Israel needs to take all measures within its power to prevent and punish those involved with inciting genocide against Palestinians in the Gaza Strip. In response to these accusations Netanyahu replied, "Like every country, Israel has an inherent right to defend itself. The vile attempt to deny Israel this fundamental right is blatant discrimination against the Jewish state, and it is justly rejected. We will continue to do what is necessary to defend our country and defend our people."

Does Israel Have the Right to Defend Itself?

From the perspective of international law and the UN, Gaza remains an Occupied Palestinian Territory subject to the Fourth Geneva Convention. According to Professor Richard Falk, the Albert G. Milbank Professor Emeritus of International Law at Princeton University, "This means that Israel as Occupying Power has a primary obligation to safeguard the safety of the civilian population. It is entitled to take reasonable lawful means to restore its security in the aftermath of such an attack as October 7, but it has no international right of self-defense. Even if it had a right of self-defense, it would have no legal or moral basis for engaging in a genocidal assault, the character of which has been strongly confirmed by Israel's top leaders, Netanyahu, Gallant and President Herzog.

Professor S. Michael Lynk, Special Rapporteur for Human Rights in the Palestinian Territory confirmed that "As an occupying power, Israel does not have a right of self- defense."

Cathy Sultan

44

Intimidation

Freedom of speech on campus is often tied up in the broader culture wars playing out in American politics right now, and the recent interrogations in Congress of the presidents of UPenn, Harvard and MIT are no exception.

President Claudine Gay of Harvard was one of three university presidents to speak at December's congressional hearings on antisemitism. Snippets of the testimony quickly went viral as the presidents sidestepped pointed questions about how they would respond to calls on campus for the genocide of Jewish people.

Republicans allowed Representative Elise Stefanik (R-NY), a Harvard alum, to speak six times. She asked each president if the call for genocide against Jewish people violated harassment policies on their campuses.

President Gay responded: "There are some who have confused a right to free expression with the idea that Harvard would condone calls for violence against Jewish students. Let me be clear: calls for violence or genocide against the Jewish community, or any religious or ethnic group are vile. They have no place at Harvard, and those who threaten our Jewish students will be held to account."

To the same question, President Magill of University of Pennsylvania, responded: "If the speech becomes conduct, it can be considered harassment."

"Conduct meaning committing the act of genocide?" Stefanik fired back.

Each president, in turn, said that it depended on the context of how the call was made, leaving Stefanik to say such answers were "unacceptable."

President Magill was the first to go, stepping down in early December under pressure from donors and board members over a Palestinian literature festival she permitted on campus in the fall. Her disastrous performance at the congressional hearings only compounded donor and board member discontent making her position as president untenable. The presidents of Harvard and the University of Pennsylvania resigned within a month of what was widely deemed disastrous testimony before the committee. Republicans on the committee cheered each resignation.

Columbia University President Minouche Shafik was adept at dodging the trick questions from the Republican members of the House Committee on Education and the Workforce but her attempt to placate them touched off a maelstrom on campus that rapidly spread to colleges and universities across the country. By opting not to push back on the McCarthyism of the committee's Republicans, Shafik failed to defend "the fundamental requirements of academic freedom" in the words of a draft censure resolution that the Columbia University Senate is expected to take up—a failure that legitimizes further attacks on individual scholars and higher education generally. To demonstrate her support for Jewish students, Shafik called in the police to arrest pro-Palestinian protesters which raised the ante and triggered even more protests at Columbia and beyond.

Peter Beihart, editor-in-chief of *Jewish Currents* and *MSNBC* commentator said, on *Democracy Now* on December 11, 2023, that "This really isn't about the individual presidents. It's about the fact that given the extraordinary slaughter that's happening in Gaza, there is a movement on college campuses and across America for a ceasefire and to end American complicity in that slaughter. In response to that, the effort is now to try to limit the ability of people who want to protest US policy and support Palestinian rights from being able to organize on college campuses. So, the reason that they're going after these presidents is to try to set a precedent and bring in people who will be much tougher on restricting the ability of students and faculty and others who want to organize politically against this war in Gaza. This is what this is about.

"As for the word "intifada" used by Representative Stefanik to mean "genocide of Jews" is just nonsense. In fact, "Intifada" is a term that has been used in uprising against Arab governments. Intifada can take nonviolent forms. The first Intifada had a lot of nonviolence. The Second Intifada involved suicide bombings, which were horrifying and totally immoral. But these were uprisings in the context of oppression. It's like saying a Ukrainian uprising against Russians that also killed Russian civilians would be an attempt at Russian genocide. It makes no sense."

Omer Bartov, Professor of Holocaust and Genocide Studies at Brown University, also on the show, said, "This whole debate is so off-kilter. The terms that are being used are being misused and are not being challenged by these three presidents, who should have been better prepared, not by their lawyers, and studied the issue itself. Using the term 'from the river to the sea,' as Stefanik did, can mean all kinds of things. There are seven million Jews living between the river and the sea, and seven million Palestinians. Historically, the term 'from the river to the sea,' or Greater Israel, which means Eretz Yisrael, the land of Israel, stretched between the Jordan and the sea. In fact, for some in the traditional revisionist movement, the right wing of the Zionist party, it also means across the river, even east of the river, into what is now known as Jordan. So, to say that it is an antisemitic term or that it calls for the genocide of the Jews is nonsense."

* * *

On June 14, Israeli American Jewish scholar Raz Segal had a job offer at the University of Minnesota rescinded after he characterized the Israeli assault on Gaza as a "textbook case of genocide." In his interview with Amy Goodman on *Democracy Now*, Professor Segal said he was confirmed to lead the University's Center for Holocaust and Genocide Studies, but after two board members quit in opposition to his appointment and a smear campaign led by the pro-Israel group Jewish Community Relations Council of Minnesota and the Dakotas (JCRC), the university revoked the offer. Professor Segal said he had been targeted because of his identity as a Jew who refused the narrowing down of Jewish identity to Zionism.

He called the JCRC-led opposition a hateful campaign of lies and distortions and crude political intervention. "This was a completely legitimate hiring process in a public university. There was a public announcement of the job. There were other applicants. There were Zoom interviews. There were campus visits. There was significant community engagement during the entire process. The search committee deliberated and made a recommendation to hire me as the dean of the College of Liberal Arts. On June 5, I received an official job offer. The recession of the university's offer spells the end of the idea of free inquiry, academic freedom, of research and teaching, and all in the service of supporting an extremely violent state.

"On June 10, the interim president of the University of Minnesota sent me an email withdrawing the job offer explaining that due to the public-facing role of the Center for Holocaust and Genocide Studies and its director, community members have come forward with some concerns. And this was the reason for the withdrawal. It's important to say here that this is a crude and dangerous case of political interference in a fair and legitimate hiring process in a public university. It's completely unacceptable that a political pressure group, the JCRC of Minnesota and the Dakotas, should take the side of Zionism and the State of Israel when it is committing genocide. This should not be the defining factor in any hiring process. This might be a legitimate case of discrimination because I was targeted as an Israeli American and because of my identity as a Jew who refused the narrowing down of Jewish identity to Zionism and unconditional support of Israel. The JCRC claims to speak for all Jews in the Twin

49

Cities which is blatantly false. I've received hundreds of emails in support of my appointment, and they all say specifically that the JCRC does not speak for them or represent them. I also received a letter signed by scholars from around the world, including many at the University of Minnesota, who support me.

"This is a very dangerous precedent the JCRC sets, that the only way to be a Jew today is to be a Zionist and to support Israel."

The ACLU Weighs in On
Student Protests

Anthony Romero, ACLU Director and David Cole, ACLU Legal Director recently wrote a letter to college and university presidents on student protests saying that "We understand that as leaders of your campus communities, it can be extraordinarily difficult to navigate the pressures you face from politicians, donors and faculty and students alike. But, as you fashion responses to the activism of your students, it is essential that you do not sacrifice principles of academic freedom and free speech that are core to the educational mission of your represented institutions. The First Amendment compels public universities and colleges to respect free speech rights. And while the constitution does not apply directly to private institutions, academic freedom and free inquiry require that similar principles guide private institutions. In the spirit of offering constructive solutions for a way forward, we offer five basic guardrails to ensure freedom of speech and academic freedom while protecting against discriminatory harassment and disruptive conduct.

1. University administrators must not single out specific viewpoints however offensive they may be to some members of the community. Viewpoint neutrality is essential be it harassment directed at individuals because of their race, ethnicity or religion. But general calls for a Palestinian state from the river to the sea or defenses of Israel's assault on Gaza, even if many listeners find these messages deeply offensive, cannot be prohibited or punished by a university that respects free speech principles.

2. Both public and private universities are bound by civil rights laws that guarantee all students equal access to education, including Title VI of the Civil Rights Act. While racist and offensive, speech is constitutionally protected. Antisemitic or anti-Palestinian speech targeted at individuals cannot be tolerated. Impassioned views about Israel or Palestine are not discrimination and should be protected. One can criticize Israel's actions without being antisemitic. And by the same token, one can support Israel's actions in Gaza and condemn Hamas without being anti-Muslim.

3. Universities can announce and enforce reasonable time and place restrictions on protest activity to ensure that essential college functions can be continued but they must leave ample

room for students to express themselves.

4. College administrators should involve police only as a last resort, after all other efforts have been exhausted.

5. Campus leaders must resist the pressures placed on them by politicians, be they Democrats or Republicans, seeking to exploit campus tensions to advance their own notoriety or partisan agendas. Recent congressional hearings have featured disgraceful attacks by members of Congress on academic freedom and freedom of speech. Universities must stand up to such intimidation and defend the principles of academic freedom so essential to their integrity and mission.

The Degraded Status
of Palestinians

According to a post on Mondoweiss dated June 9, the distain of Palestinians is consistent throughout the American establishment. *Variety* reported this week that a Hollywood marketing guru warned her employees that they should hit "pause on working with any celebrity or influencer or tastemaker posting against Israel as that simply was not true. While Jews are devastated by the loss of innocent lives in Gaza, we are feeling immense fear over the rising Jew hatred all over the world." *Variety* reported that her company is "a fixture on red carpets and is at the forefront of brand integration with celebrities" and the leading talent agencies.

* * *

The special degraded status for Palestinians has become an area of study for Palestinian intellectuals. Rabea Eghbariah, a human rights lawyer and doctoral student at Harvard, wrote a lengthy legal argument for a new term for the Palestinian condition. In his 2,000-word essay he argued that "Israel's assault on Gaza should be evaluated within and beyond the legal framework of genocide.

"The law does not possess the language that we desperately need to accurately capture the totality of the Palestinian condition. From occupation to apartheid and genocide, the most legal concepts rely on abstraction and analogy to reveal facets of subordination." He offered the idea of "Nakba" as a legal concept to encompass that subordination. His argument was censored first by the Harvard Law Review, in an unprecedented move against a fully edited essay. Then, in an even more unprecedented fashion, by the Columbia Law Review, whose board of directors, which includes alumni with ties to the Biden administration, shut down the entire website when Eghbariah's piece went up. This kind of censorship would, no doubt, have also happened in a Trump administration.

Based on their research, Israeli scholars have been well represented in the pages of the magazine, but not Palestinians. In his response to the editors, Eghbariah wrote," This is discrimination. Let's not dance around it. This is outright censorship. It is dangerous and alarming."

Because of the ensuing controversy, Columbia restored the site and allowed Eghbariah's essay to be published.

This episode of censorship reveals to what level the US establishment is firmly and blindly pro-Israeli, no matter who sits in the White House or Congress. According to Phil Weiss, Editor of *Mondoweiss,* in his June 24 article, "The US Power Structure is Blindly Dedicated to Israel," the board that squashed Rabea

Eghbariah's legal theory on the Nakba included operators of the highest order: Professor Gillian Metzger, who also serves in the Justice Department's Office of Legal Counsel; Justice Department senior counsel Lewis Yelin; and Ginger Anders, a former assistant to the US Solicitor General. "We used to call people like this the ruling class. These high appointees understand what American values are, and today American values are standing by Israel even as it massacres thousands of children. These values surely have to do with the importance of Zionist donors to Joe Biden (or Trump had he been president) and universities, but go beyond that to the makeup of the US establishment. Pro-Israel voices are a significant element of corporate culture. They are a generational force. Young progressive and young Jews are rejecting Israel, but they are not in the power structure."

According to Weiss, last November two dozen leading law firms sent a letter to leading law schools, including Harvard and Columbia, staying they would not hire students from law schools that failed to crack down on antisemitism, and one of those firms, David Polk, rescinded job offers to three students who had taken part in pro-Palestinian protests. The letter read:

"We look to you to ensure your students who hope to join our firms after graduation are prepared to be an active part of workplace communities that have zero tolerance policies for any form of discrimination or harassment, much less the kind that has been taking place on some law school campuses."

What the Columbia story tells us is that pro-Israel ideology is enmeshed in the US corporate power structure. Many of the billionaire class are in their 60s or more, and are dedicated to a country committing war crimes, but they are vanishing.

"For a younger generation, Israel is increasingly defined by its treatment of Palestinians, particularly under the last twenty years of right-wing governments led by Netanyahu, and for them, Israel is no longer seen as top dog."

Acceptance of apartheid, ethnic cleansing and unending massacres are finally becoming controversial matters, particularly in the Democratic base.

In his article, "Academia is Only as Free as Powerful Donors Allow It to Be," Johnathan Cook wrote, "Our public debates are rigged to avoid topics that would be difficult for western elites to counter, like their current support for genocide in Gaza. But the very reason we have a genocide in Gaza is because lots of other debates we should have had decades ago have not been allowed to take place, including the one Eghbariah was trying to raise.

"If even the academic community is so browbeaten by donors and the political establishment that they dare not allow serious academic debate, even of a legal concept, what hope is there that politicians and the media, equally dependent on big money and ever more sensitive to the public pressure of lobbies, are going to perform any better.

"University complicity in the Gaza genocide, brought out of the shadows by the campus protests, highlights how academic institutions are tightly integrated into the political and commercial ventures of the Western establishments."

The universities' crackdown on the student encampments, denying them any right to peacefully protest complicity in genocide by the very institutions to which they pay enormous fees, underscores the fact that universities exist only to maintain the semblance of free and open debate, but not its substance. Debate is allowed only when controlled and policed. But the very reason we have genocide in Gaza is because the debates about occupation of Palestinian land we should have had decades ago have not been allowed to take place, including Eghbariah's thesis, that the Nakba that began in 1948 has continued ever since for the Palestinian people. In the decades that followed there were meaningless "peace negotiations," but never any accountability, no truth and reconciliation process like the one that took place in South Africa, ending that country's apartheid regime. The western establishments still furiously avoid that debate seventy-six years later.

**

Congressional intimidation has not only been directed to university presidents. Such tactics have also been applied to the International Criminal Court after Karim Khan announced on May 20, 2024 his intent to seek the arrest of Israeli Prime Minister Benjamin Netanyahu and Defense Minister Yoav Gallant on charges of war crimes and crimes against humanity. According to Netanyahu, "the charges are baseless, outrageous and illegitimate." Khan simultaneously announced his intent to bring charges against Hamas' leaders for their October 7 attack on Israel, "outrageously drawing a moral equivalency between the two," according to Netanyahu.

When the chief prosecutor of the ICC announced he was seeking arrest warrants against Israeli and Hamas leaders, he issued a warning: "I insist that all attempts to impede, intimidate or improperly influence the officials of this court must cease immediately."

According to Kenneth Roth, former head of Human Rights Watch, Israel has waged a nearly decade-long campaign of intimidation against the ICC to stop possible war crimes prosecution of Israeli officials. A joint investigation by *The Guardian* and the Israeli *+972 Magazine* revealed that Israeli surveilled, hacked, smeared and threatened top ICC officials including chief prosecutor Karim Khan and his predecessor, Fatou Bensouda. The former head of the Mossad, Yossi Cohen, is said to have personally threatened Bensouda and her family. Four sources confirmed that Bensouda had briefed a small group of senior ICC officials about Cohen's attempts to sway her, amid concerns about the increasingly persistent and threatening nature of his behavior. According to accounts shared with ICC officials, Cohen is alleged to have told her, "You should help us and let us take care of you. You don't want to be getting into things that could compromise your security or that of your family." These revelations came to light after Khan announced he was seeking arrest warrants for both the leaders of Israeli and Hamas.

According to Amy Goodman on Democracy Now, a *Haaretz* article dated May 30, had planned to publish details about the Israeli intelligence operations against the ICC two years ago, but an Israeli security official blocked publication. The *Haaretz* reporter Gur Megiddo said he was summoned to the office of an Israeli security official and was told if he published the story, he would, "suffer the consequences and get to know the interrogation rooms of the Israeli security authorities from the inside."

The surveillance by the ICC provided Israel's prime minister with advance knowledge of the prosecutor's intentions. A recent intercepted communication suggested that Khan wanted to issue arrest warrants against Israelis but was under tremendous pressure from the US government not to.

Much of that pressure came from the US Congress's House of Representatives that voted by a comfortable majority on June 4 to impose sanctions on the ICC following its decision to seek arrest warrants for Netanyahu and Galant.

These arrest warrants were only made possible because on April 1, 2015, Palestine became the 123rd member state of the ICC. By doing so, Palestine granted the ICC jurisdiction over crimes committed in the Palestinian Occupied Territories, which included East Jerusalem, the West Bank and the Gaza Strip. Both the Israel and the US Congress threatened to cut off tax revenues for the Palestinian Authority if they joined the ICC, but on whose authority?

According to the 1994 Paris Protocol, tax revenues collected by Israel on behalf of the PA were to be transferred to them monthly. The protocol was meant to manage the economic relationship between Israel and the Palestinian territories until a final peace settlement was reached. Approved in the wake of the Oslo Accords, this protocol was meant to end within five years. Thirty years later, the financial settlement continues to give Israel a disproportionate leverage over not only the PA's financial affairs, but the wherewithal to blackmail and punish the

PA whenever Israel deems the PA has acted in bad faith, and that includes the PA's membership in the ICC as its 135th member that enabled the ICC to issue the arrest warrants for Netanyahu and Gallant.

The tax revenue collected by Israel on behalf of the PA amounts to around $188 million each month, and accounts for 64 percent of the PA's total revenue. A large portion of this is used to pay the salaries of the estimated 150,000 PA employees working in the West Bank and Gaza despite it having no jurisdiction over the Strip. On November 3, the Israel security cabinet voted to withhold a total of $275 million in Palestinian tax revenue, including cash collected for prior months that were still with Tel Aviv.

Under terms set by Israel's cabinet on June 23, seven months later, the monthly revenue previously allocated to PA staff in Gaza would instead be transferred to a Norwegian-based trust account. However, that money cannot be released by the fund to pay workers in Gaza without permission from Israel. In January 2023, the newly formed Israeli government of Netanyahu, seen as the most far-right coalition government in the country's history, decided to withhold an additional $39 million in tax revenues from the PA following the authority's decision to ask the ICJ to rule on the legality of Israel's decades-long occupation.

Israel's withholding of public funds due the PA has had a devastating effect on the PA's economy. It owes billions in internal debt to local banks, hospitals, medical companies and the private sector. In 2021, the PA's financial crisis, exacerbated by Israel's periodic refusal to pay the PA its total tax revenue, forced it to reduce all salaries by 25 percent. In addition to this hardship, Israel suspended the work permits of some 130,000- day workers from the occupied West Bank after October 7.

The charges brought forth by the ICC against Netanyahu and Galant were long overdue. Judge Fatou Bensouda opened a preliminary examination into crimes committed in Palestine on January 16, 2015, and the State of Palestine referred the situation for investigation on May 15, 2018. Over the course of the preliminary examination, Palestinian human rights organizations and victims made submissions in which they set forth war crimes and crimes against humanity committed by Israeli officials, including the 2014 military offensive on Gaza, the Great March of Return, the settlement expansions in East Jerusalem and the West Bank, and the multiple Israeli sieges on Gaza. On December 20, 2019, the prosecutor concluded that there was a reasonable basis to proceed with an investigation into war crimes and crimes against humanity committed on the territory of Palestine that includes the Gaza Strip, the West Bank and East Jerusalem, and asked the Pre-Trial Chamber to confirm the scope of the territorial jurisdiction of the Court. The Pre-Trial Chamber invited victims to submit observations on the prosecutor's request, and Center for Constitutional Rights attorney Katherine Gallagher made a submission on behalf of twenty Palestinian victims of persecution from all parts of Palestine and the diaspora. On April 29, 2020, the Center for Constitutional Rights joined more than 180 Palestinian, regional, and international human rights organizations in signing an open letter to the ICC prosecutor expressing support for the opening of an investigation without delay.

The US does not recognize the ICC even though it participated in its creation. On a bipartisan vote, Congress passed a draconian piece of legislation called the American Service Members Protection Act that strictly limits the US's ability to cooperate with the court so none of its servicemen, particularly those who served in Afghanistan and Iraq, can be charged and remanded to the court for crimes committed during armed conflict.

The ICC is not to be confused with the International Criminal Court of Justice (ICJ), the judicial arm of the United Nations. The ICJ settles legal disputes between nation states and issues advisory opinions upon request by UN entities. At present 123 nations have ratified the Rome Statute and are members of the ICC Assembly of States Parties. While the US played a central role in the establishment of the Rome Statute that lead to the creation of the ICC, it is not a State Party.

The Role of the Media
in This Conflict

Has the US media fairly covered the current conflict? According to recent revelations it is possible that US newspapers like the *New York Times,* The *Washington Post* and the *LA Times* may have demonstrated clear bias in their coverage of the Gaza conflict. According to *Mondoweiss,* stories of atrocities on October 7 have been used to justify the ongoing assault on Gaza. Several of these high-profile claims have been based on unreliable witnesses or fabricated entirely.

The Israeli government-affiliated "Association of Rape Crisis Centers (ARCC) maintains that Hamas combatants carried out a campaign of systematic and intentional rape on October 7. Despite the AP's acknowledgment that the report "did not specify the number of cases it had documented or identify any victims, even anonymously," and that the authors "declined to say whether they had spoken to victims." Yet, dozens of mainstream outlets have presented its findings as incontrovertible fact of rape. Among the papers most frequently cited source is a *New York Times* report by Jeffrey Gettleman purporting to detail how Hamas weaponized sexual violence on October 7. The *Times* article was based on some 150 interviews conducted by Pulitzer Prize-winning reporter Jeffrey Gettleman, along with Anat Schwartz and Adam Sella. The story concluded that Hamas fighters engaged in systematic rape and sexual violence against Israeli women. The article focused on one central story, that of Gal Abdush, who was described in the article as "The Woman in the Black Dress." The story was undermined as soon as it was published by the Abdush family who said there was no proof their daughter had been raped, and that the *New York Times* interviewed them on false pretenses. The report centered around a video that when released showed a distant, indistinct image that revealed nothing at all. The *Times* stated that the Israeli police used the video as evidence but there is no trace of the video on the internet despite the *Times* claim that it went viral.

On December 29 the Israeli website *Ynet* published an interview with Etti Brakha, Gal Abdush's mother. In the interview Gal's mother said her daughter had not been raped. On January 1, Nissim Abdush, Gal's brother-in-law appeared on Israeli Channel thirteen in which he said he had spoken to his brother who was next to Gal's body. He never mentioned any sexual assault.

* * *

ZAKA, the ultra-Orthodox "rescue" group introduced allegations that Hamas beheaded babies, cut fetuses from pregnant women, among a myriad of other accusations.

ZAKA has since been lambasted in Israeli media for mishandling evidence from the October 7 attacks. Shortly after ZAKA made these allegations *Haaretz* reported that Yehuda Meshi-Zahav, the founder of ZAKA, was charged for alleged sexual offenses, including rape and exploitation of women, men and children.

Israeli security agencies and UN examiners were unable to find any videos or photos of sexual assaults on October 7. An article in *Haaretz* in April, confirmed that "from inquiries put to three bodies in the defense establishment, it emerges that the intelligence material collected by the police and the intelligence bodies, including footage from terrorists' body cameras, does not contain visual documentation of any acts of rape."

* * *

The UN Independent Commission of Inquiry headed by Pramila Patten also reviewed thousands of photos and videos provided by the Israeli government and concluded in its report published in March that "in the medicolegal assessment of available photos and videos, no tangle indications of rape could be identified. Patten's team faced "active attempts by Israeli authorities to obstruct the Commission's access to information related to sexual violence. Such measures included instructing medical professionals note to cooperate with the Commission."

* * *

On June 17, Vice President Kamala Harris hosted a White House screening of Sheryl Sandberg's *Screams before Silence*, a film which included "confession" footage of Palestinians who support Tel Aviv's October 7 mass rape accusations. In promoting the event, Congresswoman Debbie Wasserman Schultz claimed she saw videos of a rape in progress, footage that Israeli and international investigators have determined does not exist. The film's screening is a collaboration between the White House Gender Policy Council and several Israeli lobby groups, according to *Jewish Insider.* In an article promoting the White House screening, *The Jerusalem Post* asserted that the sexual assaults committed by Hamas prompted former Meta CEO Sandberg to make the documentary which was directed by Anat Stalinsky, an Israeli film maker.

* * *

According to a leaked memo dated April 15 and published in *The Intercept* by Jeremy Scahill, the *New York Times* instructed journalists covering Israel's war on Gaza Strip to restrict the use of the words, "genocide" and "ethnic cleansing" and to avoid using the phrase "occupied territory" when describing Palestinian land. The memo, written by *Times* editor Susan Wessling, international editor Philip Pan and their deputies "offers guidance about some terms and other issues we have grappled with since the start of the conflict in October." The memo also instructed reporters not to use the word Palestine except on rare occasions, and to steer clear of the term "refugee camps" to describe areas of Gaza historically settled by displaced Palestinians expelled from other parts of Palestine during previous wars.

While the document was meant as an outline for maintaining objective journalistic principles, several *Times* staffers told *The Interc*ept that some of its comments show evidence of the paper's deference to

Israeli narratives. On the term "Palestine," a widely used name for both the territory and the U.N. recognized state, the *Times* memo contains blunt instructions: "Do not use in datelines, routine texts or headlines, except in very rare cases such as when the U.N. General Assembly elevated Palestine to a nonmember observer state, or references to historic Palestine. "

In an analysis in January of the *New York Times, Washington Post* and *Los Angeles Times, The Intercept* found that the major newspapers reserved terms like "slaughter," "massacre," and "horrific" almost exclusively for Israeli citizens killed by Palestinians, rather than for Palestinian civilians killed in Israeli attacks. The analysis found that as of November 24, the *New York Times* had described Israeli deaths as a "massacre" on fifty-three occasions and those of Palestinians just once. The ratio for the use of "slaughter" was twenty-two to one, even as the documented number of Palestinians killed climbed by large numbers.

Of the three victims specifically singled out by the *Times* in an article published in December, which alleged that Hamas had deliberately weaponized sexual violence during the October 7 attacks, referencing Jeffrey Gettleman's Words without Screams article, Michael Paikin, spokesperson for Kibbutz Be'eri said there were no victims of sexual assault. "The Sharabi girls were shot but were not subjected to sexual abuse." Paikin also disputed the graphic and highly detailed claims of the Israeli special forces paramedic who served as the source for the allegation, which was published in the *New York Times*, The *Washington Post, CNN* and other news outlets. "It's not true. They were not sexually abused."

"We stand by the story and are continuing to report on the issue of sexual violence on October 7," *Times* spokesperson Danielle Rhoades Ha told The Intercept. A spokesperson for the Israeli governments, Eylon Levy, played a lead role in connecting the story to international news outlets.

Social Media and Its Impact
on the Narrative

Social media has transformed the way we see the world. In the case of Gaza, the conflict is live-streamed, twenty-four seven. TikTok, X, Instagram and Facebook users post online from both sides, fighting to win the social media war and influence public opinion. Main stream media, which has historically supported Israel, no longer has a monopoly on information dissemination. How has this affected public opinion?

"It's particularly relevant in this instance," David Patrikarakos, war correspondent and author, told Desiree Adib in her November 24 article "Amid Israel-Hamas Conflict, 'Information war' Plays Out on Social Media." "The military battle with Hamas and Israel is predetermined. Hamas cannot defeat the IDF and the IDF cannot defeat Hamas. So, you have a wider battle, let's call it an information war."

Citing a disparity between pro-Israel and pro-Palestinian social media posts, Max Boot, a military historian and foreign policy analysist, told ABC News he believes, "Israel is losing the information war because it's a battle of victimhood." A recent study by *The Washington Post* found that the number of pro-Palestinian hashtags used on the TikTok, Instagram and Facebook platforms have dwarfed pro-Israel hashtags since Hamas attack Israel on October 7. TikTok said those hashtag numbers lacked context since many users come from the Middle East and Southeast Asia. On Facebook, *The Post* found that the #freepalestine hashtag was used thirty-seven times more than the #standwithisrael hashtag and twenty-six times more on Instagram. Hamas' attack on Israel was brutal and horrifying but with ongoing Israeli retaliatory attacks in Gaza being played out on social media, day after day, the narrative has changed. "The sympathy of a lot of people in the world has shifted away from Israelis," Max Boot said. "The IDF holding press conferences is very different from seeing the aftermath of the attacks on Gaza. Online what speaks powerfully is images."

Inside Gaza, citizen journalists, filmmakers, mothers, poets, writers, students and photographers posting on social media say they've seen their engagement grow as the fighting rages on. "The impact is huge. That's the power of the iPhone, arming people to be media outlets for the democratization of information," Valerie Wirtschafter, a fellow from the Brookings Institute studying the impact of emerging technology, told ABC News. "At the core, to be able to document and share is very important, especially in places that journalists don't have access to because everyday citizens are living there. The challenge is that there is such a high volume of information that the footage gets muddled with other videos and it's leading to an overarching sense of mistrust."

But is that true? TikTok critics are being slammed for their pro-Palestinian hashtags, but they aren't alone, according to Drew Harwell in his November 13, 2023 article "TikTok was Slammed for Its pro-Palestinian Hashtags. The app's critics in Washington say the difference in views between pro-Israel and pro-Palestinian hashtags is proof of mass brainwashing, but Facebook and Instagram show the same imbalance." Not to be deterred, both congressional Republicans and Democrats continue to repeat their long-running demands for a nationwide ban on TikTok, highlighting a data point they say is proof of the app's sinister underpinnings. That gap offers evidence that the app, owned by the Chinese tech giant ByteDance, was being used to boost propaganda and brainwash American viewers, even though Facebook and Instagram showed similar gap posts. On Facebook, the #freepalestine hashtag was found on more than eleven million posts, thirty-nine times more than those with @standwithisrael. On Instagram, the pro-Palestinian hashtag was found on six million posts, twenty-six times more than the pro-Israel hashtag. These figures, from November 2023, undercut the argument that has become central to the latest wave of anti-TikTok rage in Washington, that the Chinese government is manipulating TikTok's algorithm to play up pro-Palestinian viewpoints and that the app, which has 150 million users in the US, should be banned nationwide.

Given the evidence, it is hard not to conclude that the TikTok ban is being pursued because of its impact in empowering voices that were previously marginalized, a situation that is no doubt detrimental to the official US narrative. Democracy requires an informed citizenry that can hold its government accountable. Foreign social media platforms such as TikTok have torn down the barrier between Americans and the atrocities their government carries out abroad, using their tax dollars. The bottom line is that in the US and mainstream media, which has historically supported Israel, no longer has the monopoly on information dissemination.

In their masterpieces *Manufacturing Consent: The Political Economy of the Mass Media* and *The Political Economy of Human Rights,* Noam Chomsky and Edward S. Herman demonstrate that the US media serve as effective ideological institutions, propagating the interests of those in power through subtle mechanisms of persuasion and self-censorship. Both authors assert that this is particularly evident in issues involving significant US economic and political interests, where the media often function as state propaganda agencies. Removal of TikTok would suppress pro-Palestinian voices.

At the McCain Institute's 2024 Sedona Forum event on May 3, and reported on in Common Dreams on May 6 by Julia Conley, Senator Mitt Romney spoke with US Secretary of State Antony Blinken about what one critic called "the incredible mask-off moment," with the two officials speaking openly about the US government's long-term attempts to provide public relations work for Israel in defense of its policies in the Occupied Palestinian Territories and its push to ban TikTok in order to shut down Americans' access to unfiltered news about the Israeli assault on Gaza.

Senator Romney asked Blinken why Israel's PR has been so bad. "The world is screaming about Israel, why aren't they screaming about Hamas? Instead, it's the other way around. Typically the Israelis are good at PR. What's happened here. How have they, and we, been so ineffective at communicating the realities there?"

Blinken replied, "Americans, two-thirds of whom want the Biden administration to push for a permanent ceasefire, and 57 percent of whom disapprove of President Biden's approach to the war, are on an intravenous feed of information with new impulses, inputs every millisecond. And of course the way this has played out in social media has dominated the narrative. We can't discount that fact, but I think it also has a very challenging effect on the narrative."

Social media has provided the public with an unvarnished look at the scale of Israel's attack, with users learning the history of Israeli aggression against the Palestinian people and about the stories of people living in Gaza, and seeing the destruction of hospitals, universities and civilian infrastructure, not to mention the hundreds of victims found in mass graves. As the conflict lingers on, it is not just US students who are expressing strong opposition to Israel's actions. Human rights groups across the globe have demanded an end to the Biden administration's support for Israel. Josep Borrell, the EU's High Representative for Foreign Affairs and Security Policies, lambasted Biden for claiming concern about the safety of Palestinians while continuing to arm Israel, while leaders of Ireland and Spain have led calls for arms embargo on Israel. Neither Romney nor Blinken mentioned whether they thought social media and bad PR had pushed international leaders to make similar demands to those college students.

"The conversation," said *Intercept* journalist Ryan Grim, "was an incredible historical document showing how the US government views its role in the Middle East, to mediate between Israel and the public to keep people from having a direct look at what's happening."

"Romney's comments betray a general bipartisan disinterest in engaging Israel's conduct in Gaza on its own terms, preferring instead to complain about protesters, interrogate university presidents, and, apparently, muse about social media's role in boosting pro-Palestinian activism," wrote Beri Metzner at *The New Republic.* As Israel moves closer to a catastrophic invasion of Rafah, having already banned *Al Jazeera from* the country, Romney and Blinken would be wise to consider whether TikTok is the real problem." Entrepreneur James Rosen-Birch added that "Mitt Romney flat-out asked Antony Blinken in public why the US is not doing a better job manufacturing consent for Israel."

* * *

Over the last eight months, stories of atrocities, sometimes cobbled together from unreliable eyewitnesses, sometimes fabricated entirely, have made their way to heads of state and been used to justify Israel's military violence. To date, 85 percent of Gazans have been displaced. As many as 38,000 have been killed (not counting the unknown numbers still under rubble). Seventy percent of Gaza's homes are flattened. Some one hundred journalists have been killed and every university in Gaza has been destroyed. Two hundred doctors who worked in Gaza hospitals are unaccounted for. To date, we know that two were tortured to death by Shin Bet interrogators. *Middle East Eye* reported in a June 19 article that Doctor Iyad Rantisi, director of Kamal Adwan Hospital's maternity department, died in November at an Israeli interrogation facility six days after he had been abducted from the Gaza Strip. In April, Palestinian surgeon and professor of orthopedics, Dr. Adnan al-Bursh, was killed by torture according to the Palestinian Prisoners' Society while in Israeli detention. Israeli forces have killed nearly 500 Palestinian medical workers and detained 310 over the last eight months. Rantisi's death was reported first by *Haaretz* and then by *Al Jazeera Arabic.* According to *Haaretz,* Rantisi died at an interrogation facility run by the Shin Bet, Israel's internal intelligence agency. A court in Israel has banned the publication of details about his death for six months. Isael has destroyed Gaza's health system through its constant attacks on hospitals, ambulances and doctors by air strikes, detentions and denial of medical equipment. According *Middle East Eye*, Israeli authorities have also been accused of widespread and systematic torture and abuse of Palestinian detainees and prisoners since October 7. This has led to the death of some sixty Palestinians, forty of them from the Gaza Strip, including thirty-eight who died in the notorious detention camp at the Sde Teiman military base.

In a statement released on May 23 by the U.N. Special Rapporteur on Torture, Alice Jill Edwards said, "Official downgrading of conditions in certain places of detention is not acceptable. At all times, the minimum international standards must be adhered to. How we treat others during moments of crisis is a sign of how much we have internalized human rights," she said. "No circumstances, however exceptional, can ever justify torture or ill-treatment. The Israeli authorities must investigate all complaints and reports of torture or ill-treatment promptly, impartially, effectively and transparently. Those responsible at all levels, including commanders, must be held accountable, while victims have a right to reparation and compensation."

As reported in the *Palestine Chronicle* on June 6, two journalists from *the New York Times* spent three months interviewing both Israeli soldiers who work at Sde Teiman and Palestinians who were detained there. One of the journalists after visiting the site, provided additional insight into Israel's policy of systematic torture and abuse since October 7, challenging the Israeli government's repeated claims that it operates according to accepted international practices and laws. Sde Teiman, a makeshift interrogation center has become a major focus of accusations that the Israeli military has mistreated detainees, including people determined to have no ties to Hamas or other armed groups. Of the 4,000 detainees housed at Sde Teiman since October, twenty-five have died. The testimonies in the U.N. report correlate with those collected by the *New York Times* which included allegations of rape, including with metal rods. One male detainee died after experiencing anal rape as a form of sexual torture.

According to *Palestine Chronicle,* one thousand Palestinians have disappeared from Gaza.

Israel's Propaganda Campaign

The Guardian reported on June 24 that Israel was covertly funding a massive propaganda campaign to target the US public, including through the passage of legislation to restrict US citizens' right to free speech when criticizing Israel and its ongoing war on Gaza. There are eighty programs already underway as part of the massive propaganda campaign known as. the "Voices of Israel." The program is funded and run by the Israeli Ministry of Diaspora Affairs, led by MK Amiichai Chikli. The program was designed to carry out what Israel calls "mass consciousness activities" targeting the US and European public. Voices of Israel is part of the latest incarnation of a sometimes-covert operation by the Israeli military to censor students, human rights groups and other critics of Israel. Known previously as Concert and before that Kela Shlomo, the campaign previously spearheaded efforts to pass "anti-BDS state laws that penalized Americans for engaging in. boycotts or other nonviolent protests against Israel. Voices of Israel works through non-profits and other entities that often do not disclose donor information.

From October 2023 through May 2024, the campaign has spent $8.6 million to target US citizens with pro-Israel propaganda.

The Institute for the Study of Global Antisemitism and Policy (ISGAP) is one such organization that receives funding through the Israeli program. It recently cited its success during congressional hearings in which Harvard's Claudine Gay was grilled for allowing pro-Palestinian protests on campus.

"These hearings were a result of our report that all these universities, beginning with Harvard, are taking a lot of money from Qatar," bragged Natan Sharansky, the ISGAP chair."

Another group tied to Voices of Israel and the Ministry of Diaspora Affairs campaign is CyberWell, a pro-Israel "anti-disinformation" group led by former Israeli military intelligence officials. CyberWell has established itself as an official "trusted partner" to TikTok and Meta, allowing it to help screen and edit content. A recent CyberWell report called for Meta to suppress the popular slogan "From the river to the sea, Palestine will be free."

The Guardian noted, "One struggles to find a parallel in terms of a foreign country's influence over American political debate."

US-based organizations that produce propaganda or lobby to influence US citizens are required by law to register as foreign agents, but none of these groups have registered under the Foreign Agents Registration Act (FARA).

"Apparently there's a built-in assumption that there's nothing weird about viewing the US as sort of an open field for Israel to operate in, that there are no limitations," said Lara Friedman, president of the Foundation for Middle East Peace.

The IDF's Response to October 7

There are growing concerns about the Israeli Defense Force's response to the October 7 Hamas attack. This includes intelligence failures in the lead-up to the attack as well as reports of Israeli troops killing Israeli civilians when they opened fire with tanks on homes taken over by Hamas militants. *Haaretz* reported that a group of family members were killed in the home of Pesi Cohen in Kibbutz Be'eri and demanded a probe into how they were killed. In a recent interview, Brigadier General Barak Hiram told the *New York Times* that he ordered an Israeli tank commander to fire on a home where Hamas fighters were holding fifteen Israeli hostages, and "to break in even at the cost of civilian casualties.' Hiram was also handed a disciplinary reprimand by his chief of staff for blowing up the main building of Israa University in the Gaza Strip in January without proper authorization.

A *Haaretz* reported on November 18 that an Israeli police investigation into the Hamas attack on the Nova music festival near the Gaza border on October 7 revealed that an Israeli attack helicopter killed some of the attendees.

The helicopter arrived on the scene from the Ramat David base and fired at Hamas fighters killing some attendees. Some 364 people were killed. The Israeli military and rescue services had previously claimed that 260 Israelis were killed at the festival, all by Hamas, in a deliberate massacre but this is the first acknowledgment that Israeli forces killed some of their own. A similar attack occurred in Sderot, on the Gaza/Israeli border when Hamas fighters had taken over the local police station. Both the Hamas fighters and prisoners were killed when an Israeli army tank fired at the police station killing everyone and then bulldozed the station. *Haaretz* reported that "There is a growing assessment in the security establishment that Hamas did not know in advance about the Nova festival near Kibbutz Re'im and only arrived there once they discovered the event. '

It is unclear how many Israelis were killed by Hamas fighters. They had planned to take as many Israelis as possible, both soldiers and civilians, back to Gaza, and how many were killed by Israeli forces. Israeli spokesperson, Mark Regev, acknowledged that 200 of the alleged victims were Hamas. Their bodies were so badly burned that Israeli authorities could not initially identify them. The majority of the 3,000 attendees managed to escape.

The Hannibal Directive

There is no room for doubt that the IDF killed Israeli civilians during the events of October 7. Crucial to this assessment is the role of the Hannibal Directive, an order with a forty-year history that prioritizes destruction of the enemy over the safety of prisoners of war. October 7 appears to have marked the first time this directive has been extended beyond endangering captured soldiers The secretive Hannibal Directive is named after an ancient Carthaginian general who poisoned himself rather than be captured alive by the Roman Empire. These revelations came to light in an article written by Ronan Bergman and Yoav Zitun, two journalists with extensive sources inside Israel's military and intelligence establishment. Their article, written in Hebrew, was not translated into English by its publisher, *Yedioth Ahronoth*. However, the full English version was translated by Dena Shunra for *The Electronic* Intifada and is available on their website. The journalists wrote that "it is not clear at this stage how many of the captives were killed due to the Hannibal Directive," but some seventy vehicles driven by Palestinian fighters returning to Gaza, some of which contained Israeli captives, were blown up by Israeli helicopter gunships, drones and tanks.

The Israeli government denies the use of this directive. However, at midday on October 7 Israel's supreme military command ordered all units "to prevent the capture of Israeli hostages by any means possible., even by firing on them." These orders resulted in the deaths of Israeli citizens, often with the full knowledge of the military unit perpetrating the act. The goal of the Hannibal Directive, when executed, is to prevent Israelis from being taken captive by resistance fighters who would then use them as leverage for prisoner exchange deals. Hamas has claimed, all along, that it targeted military bases and outposts, and that their goal was to capture rather than kill Israeli civilians and kill or capture Israeli soldiers, an act justified by international law which gives the occupied the legitimate right to fight the occupier. At this time, without an official inquiry, it is impossible to say how many Israeli civilians were killed by Hamas and how many were killed by the Hannibal Directive. Based on interviews with those present, the new article says that top officers at Israel's underground military headquarters in Tel Aviv on 7 October admitted that it was shocked that the Gaza Division was overpowered. Why was this a surprise when it was well known that many of the soldiers usually posted along the Gaza Strip had been transferred to the West Bank to oversee Israeli settler activity?

Underscoring the need for an inquiry are the testimonies of two escaped hostages who confirm they were fired on by IDF forces while they were being taken to Gaza. In another instance, a hostage negotiation in Kibbutz Be'eri between Hamas and Israeli police and IDF forces turned into a massacre when a tank fired two shells in the house, killing nearly everyone inside. The only hostage inside the house who survived confirmed that many of the other hostages inside were killed by the IDF's decision to fire on the house. In another instance, it was Col. Golan Vach who confirmed the use of a tank to destroy a building, killing everyone inside. In Kibbutzim Be'eri and Kfar Aza both Israeli tank and helicopter fire were used. The aftermath of tank shelling looks very different from arson and small arms fire, which was what Hamas fighters used. There is more rubble, and less soot. In Be'eri, where fighting was most intense, half the damage came from munitions impacts and the other half from arson.

* * *

A June 20 report in *Haaretz* entitled, " Women Soldiers Who Warned of a Pending Hamas Attack —and Were Ignored," exposed another failure. Fifteen Israeli Defense Forces (IDF) spotters, all women, at the Nahal Oz lookout base along the Gaza border, warned their superiors that something unusual was happening. The two who survived the brutal attack at their post are convinced that if it had been men sounding the alarm, the attack would not have happened. These women spotters were able to estimate the number of hostages Hamas intended to kidnap at 200 to 250. Hama stook 251 hostages. They watched Hamas fighters carrying out exercises, including mock-up raids on Israeli towns and military posts. They knew when Hamas fighters gathered for meals, when they prayed, every detail of their daily activities, including how to drive vehicles across the border, murder Israeli soldiers, take over army bases, dismantle cameras on the border fence and then cross back into Gaza with hostages. As the two survivors told Israeli investigative journalist Roni Singer on public broadcaster Kan, they are not only dealing with loss of their friends, the trauma of the day and physical injuries, but something much worse. Time and time again they told their commanders what they had witnessed only to be told their findings were meaningless. One high ranking Israeli officer who visited Nahal Oz base prior to the attack was explicit. "I don't want to hear another word about this nonsense. You are our eyes, not the head that needs to make decisions about the information. If you nudge me again about this, you will stand trial."

Gideon Leavy, a journalist at *Haaretz* commented on these findings. "The stories about how these soldiers were so contemptibly and consistently ignored by older, more experienced men are so astounding that they are already the basis of some of the conspiracy theories surrounding the events of October 7. Because why would a high-tech military, an intelligence superpower, build sophisticated defense systems, spend billions on them just to then do absolutely nothing with the information they collected?"

The Origins of Hamas

The history of Hamas begins in 1973. That year a quadriplegic Palestinian by the name of Ahmed Yassin founded a charity called the Mujama al-Oslamiya in Gaza. Yassin was born in 1936 in a village near Ashkelon in what was then Mandatory Palestine, administered by Britian after World War I. That village was one of more than five hundred that was obliterated by Israeli forces in 1948 to create the State of Israel. The UN ceasefire left the West Bank and Gaza outside the Green Line that still defined the territory of Israel proper. It was then that Yassin fled to Gaza where he had relatives. Yassin attended Al Azhar University in Cairo where he came under the influence of the Muslim Brotherhood, a religious and political movement in Egypt in the 1970s. During the first Intifada in 1987, the charity he founded would become Hamas, an acronym for the Arabic name Harakat al Muqawama al Islamiya, or the Movement of Islamic Resistance. Its terrorist wing carried out its first suicide bombings inside Israel in April 1993. The leading Palestinian organization, the secular Fatah, regarded Hamas as a hostile rival and it was only in 2017 when Hamas revised its doctrine that had called for the elimination of Israel, to agree to a document calling for a Palestinian state in the West Bank, Gaza and the West Bank which implied on the part of Hamas recognition of Israel within the pre-1967 border.

A critical piece of Israel's Likud's charter was its opposition to any Palestinian state. Since this was in opposition to the US's so called two-state solution, Netanyahu and his Likud party's alternative was never publicly stated. The alternative was obvious. Endless wars and military occupation while Israel usurped Palestinian land in the West Bank and East Jerusalem and populated both with settlers who today terrorize residents of the West Bank in the hopes of driving them into neighboring Arab states so the West Bank can be annexed to Israel. When the PLO renounced armed struggle and agreed to a two-state solution the situation for Likud became more critical. Peace was the real enemy. For years various Israeli governments led by Netanyahu took an approach that divided power between the Gaza Strip and the West Bank bringing PA's Mahmoud Abbas to his knees while making moves that propped up Hamas. The idea was to prevent Abbas, or anyone else in the PA, from advancing the establishment of a Palestinian state. In this bid to cripple Abbas, Hamas was upgraded from a mere terror group to an organization with which Israel held indirect negotiations via Egypt, and one that was allowed to receive infusions of cash from abroad. Hamas was also included in discussions about increasing the number of work permits Israel granted to Gazan laborers which kept money flowing into Gaza, meaning food for families and the ability to buy basic products. When Netanyahu returned to power in 2021, he boosted work permits to an unprecedented 20,000 work permits, all the while treating the PA as a burden and Hamas as an asset. Meanwhile, since 2018, Israel has allowed suitcases holding $30 millions of Qatari cash to enter Gaza through its crossing to maintain its fragile ceasefire with Hamas. Qatar had been reluctant at first because the US and the EU had designated Hamas a terrorist organization. The emir and his advisers demanded that Netanyahu get authorization from the US for this transfer of funds. President Donald Trump made the arrangements. The approval of Secretary of the Treasury Steve Mnuchin was needed for this scheme to go forward. Mnuchin, a Wall Street wheeler-dealer before his appointment, had been embroiled in lawsuits and investigations, and likely admired Netanyahu, agreed to write a letter to the emir, which said, "The funding of Hamas would not be considered funding terror."

"Anyone who wants to thwart the establishment of a Palestinian state should support bolstering Hamas and transferring money to Hamas. This is part of our strategy, to isolate the Palestinians in Gaza from the Palestinians in the West Bank," said Netanyahu.

The idea of indirectly strengthening Hamas, while tolerating sporadic flare-ups, went up in flames on October 7.

On May 5, 2019, Gershon Hacohen, a reserve Israeli major general, told the Ynet news site, "We need to tell the truth. Netanyahu's strategy is to prevent the option of two states, so he is turning Hamas into our closest partner. Openly, Hamas is the enemy. Covertly, it's an ally."

From that time forward, Qatar sent billions of dollars to Hamas at the behest of Netanyahu. Though now he says he wants to destroy Hamas, he knows that will be impossible.

On October 24, 2023, Iris Leal, an Israeli journalist wrote in H*aaretz,* "If we do not want to show weakness, the goals of the war must be logical: a heavy blow, but not the insanity of flattening and occupying Gaza that has seized everyone. We need to rehabilitate, not spill more blood. We must concentrate our efforts on a major hostage deal and make time for the process of recovery and the de-Nazification of Israeli society. It will begin with bringing down the government and its leader and establishing a commission of inquiry for the events of October 7, the events of the black year that preceded it, and the decay of the years of Netanyahu's rule that led to them."

The catastrophe of Gaza is the result of the hubris of Netanyahu, of his cynical and devious plot to forestall all negotiations. His ability to manipulate and survive through difficult times is remarkable but with charges of bribery and fraud hanging over him is reason enough in his mind to prolong the war in Gaza or start a new front in southern Lebanon.

The Peace Deal That Never Was

Biden's Gaza peace plan announcement on May 31 was a riddle wrapped in a mystery inside an enigma," wrote James Zogby, president of the Arab American institute, in *Opinion* on June 24. In early June, in a televised speech to the nation, Biden announced a three-stage peace deal that would lead to the end of the conflict. The plan, he insisted, had already been approved by Israel and the burden was now on Hamas to accept its terms.

The first phase would entail a complete ceasefire, the withdrawal of Israeli forces from populated areas in Gaza; the release of some hostages and some bodies of hostages; the return of Palestinian civilians to their homes and a surge in humanitarian aid. The second phase would involve a permanent end to hostilities; the release of remaining living hostages; and a withdrawal of Israeli forces from Gaza. The third phase would focus on a major reconstruction plan for Gaza; and the return of the final bodies of hostages to their families, removing the final bodies.

Following Biden's announcement, Netanyahu issued a statement saying he rejected the plan. In a social media post, he noted that no actual plan to which he had agreed stipulated no end to the conflict until Hamas had been eliminated; no permanent ceasefire until all hostages are freed and victory was achieved; and no end to an Israeli security role in Gaza.

Netanyahu's June 1 statement read: "Israel's conditions for ending the war have not changed: the destruction of Hamas' military and governing capabilities, the freeing of all hostages and ensuring that Gaza no longer poses a threat to Israel. Under the proposal, Isael will continue to insist these conditions are met before a permanent ceasefire is put in place. the notion that Israel will agree to a permanent ceasefire before these conditions are fulfilled is a non-starter."

When asked to clarify the discrepancy between what Biden and Netanyahu were saying, both the White House and the State Department spokespeople appeared to accept Netanyahu's terms. On national television, US national security advisor Jake Sullivan said: "It's an Israeli proposal. The Israeli government has reconfirmed repeatedly, as recently, as today, that the proposal is still on the table, and now it's up to Hamas to accept it, and the whole world should call on Hamas to accept it." Later the State Department spokesperson said: "If Hamas was truly committed to saving the lives of its people instead of simply saving its own position, then it should accept the deal."

To confuse matters more, on June 10, the US was able to secure passage of a UN Security Council resolution that referred to the May 31 ceasefire proposal as one "which Israel accepted" and "calls on Hamas to also accept it and urges both parties to implement its terms without delay and without conditions."

Israel is not a member of the Security Council and could not vote, but its ambassador stated that Israel rejected the resolution, noting that it ran counter to his government's goal of total victory in Gaza.

Adding to the confusion, the US leaked what it said had been Israel's detailed response to the proposals put forward by the US. It differed in that it only offered a limited withdrawal in phase one and a complete withdrawal of its forces would only occur in phase two subject to negotiations, none of which were in either the Biden plan or the UN resolution. For its part, Hamas accepted the Biden plan and the UN resolution with some caveats. It insisted that the end of the ceasefire lead to permanent peace, and that there be a complete withdrawal of all Israeli forces from Gaza.

Anthony Blinken then said: "Israel accepted the proposal as it was," before adding that "Hamas could have answered with a single word: 'Yes.'"

James Zogby was right when he asked: "Why the confusion, or was it intentional deception?"

Why Did Hamas Attack
When It Did?

Though it is pure speculation at this point, there are factors that surely played a role in Hamas' thinking when it planned its October 7 attack.

1. Hamas had repeatedly warned of repercussions if Israeli forces did not stop entering, attacking worshippers and desecrating Haram al Sharif, Islam's third-holiest place in the Old City of Jerusalem. Non-Muslims are not permitted onto the site.

2. Hamas has repeatedly called for the cessation of violence against Palestinians in the West Bank. Over the last year, there have been repeated attacks on their villages, their homes and vehicles, their places of business and their olive and fruit orchards torched. Hundreds have died at the hands of the settlers.

3. Hamas has demanded the release of political prisoners in Israeli prisons, numbering close to 7,000. Their demand has repeatedly been ignored.

4. In September 2023, at the United Nations, Netanyahu showed a map of what he referred to as the New Middle East that excluded any mention of the West Bank or Gaza. *Middle East Eye* reported that Netanyahu also held up a map of "Israel in 1948," the year the modern Jewish state was established, that included the Occupied Palestinian Territories as part of Israel. Palestinian Ambassador to Germany Laith Arafeh said on social media that there is "no greater insult to every foundational principle of the U.N. than seeing Netanyahu display before the UNGA a 'map of Israel' that straddles the entire land from the river to the sea, negating Palestine and its people, then attempting to spin the audience with rhetoric about 'peace' in the region, all the while entrenching the longest ongoing belligerent occupation in today's world."

As *Middle East Eye* noted, the inclusion of Palestinian lands into Israeli maps is common among believers of the concept of Eretz Yisrael or Greater Israel, a key part of ultra-nationalist Zionism that claims that all this land belongs to a Zionist state. Earlier in the year, Bezalel Smotrich said there was "no such thing as Palestinians." The use of such maps by Israeli officials comes at a time when Netanyahu's government has taken steps that experts say amount to the *de jure* annexation of the occupied West Bank. Netanyahu also used the maps to illustrate the increasing number of Arab countries normalizing relations with Israel under the Abraham Accords brokered by former President Trump's administration. "There is no question the Abraham Accords heralded the dawn of a new age of peace, but I believe that we are at the cusp of an even more dramatic breakthrough, a historic peace between Israel and Saudi Arabia. Peace between us will truly create a new Middle East," said Netanyahu.

5. The normalization between Saudi Arabia and Israel, the dream of President Biden, excluded any mention of the Palestinians. Indeed, the Biden administration remains focused on the goal of integrating Israel into the US-led network of alliances and partnerships in the Middle East, just as it had attempted to do before October 7. Rather than trying to achieve a two-state solution, or any solution that would better the lives of the Palestinians who have lived in misery under a seventy-five year-long military occupation, the administration is working to take advantage of the current crisis for the purpose of strengthening US dominance, regardless of the consequences for the Palestinians. "Despite the fact that we say the words "two-state solution" we have never used our influence to make it happen," said Senator Van Hollen.

For all the reasons listed above, Hamas attacked on October 7. They changed the world and opened eyes to the plight of the Palestinian people.

Should We Condemn Hamas?

According to James Ray writing in *Mondoweiss* on June 5, "it is not whether we condemn Hamas but whether we condemn a settler-colonial regime that makes armed struggles necessary for survival." The question whether Palestinian armed resistance factions deserve support or criticism is also valid, For some it was easy to support the Palestinian cause when they were the perfect victim, but what about now, after October 7?

As Franz Fanon's oft-cited statement from Wretched of the Earth has made clear, national liberation, national reawakening, restoration of the nation to the Commonwealth, whatever the name use, decolonization is always a violent event and Palestine is no exception. And Palestinian resistance becomes mainstream out of necessity.

Even before Israel declared itself a state in 1948, this cycle of violence was already established. The Balfour Declaration came into existence in 1917, singling Britian's official endorsement of Zionist aspirations at the expense of the indigenous people of

Palestine. According to Ghassan Kanafani's seminal work on the 1936 Great Palestinian Revolt, by 1929, a fifth of Palestinians found themselves landless. By the 1930s, many Palestinians found themselves unemployed and economically destitute as Zionist capital, back by British laws and favorable treatment, began flowing into Palestine. These factors spurred resistance of their own variety, including the Buraq Uprising of 1929, the efforts by Palestinians to pool resources to purchase land, sporadic violence, as well as Palestinian notables lobbying for better treatment from their British overlords. This blend of violent and nonviolent efforts would all be suppressed or ultimately met with very limited success.

In 1936, when British forces murdered Syrian revolutionary figure Shaykh Izz al Din al Qasem, Palestinian popular resentment turned into a general strike, and ultimately into popular revolt, which was put down brutally by Zionist and British forces by 1939.

In 1948, Zionists ethnically cleansed more than 750,000 Palestinians from upward of 530 villages, towns and villages, killing thousands more in what the Palestinians call the Nakba, or catastrophe. Israel's ethnic cleansing campaigns continued. Palestinians rose up because of the subjugation they faced through a combination of violent and nonviolent struggle that was met with even greater violence. When Palestinians rose up, they were met with violent crackdowns, mass arrests and widespread violence. This led to the intensification of violence on their part.

In 1987 the first Intifada began in reaction to the killing of six Palestinian children by Israeli soldiers. When it ended in 1993, eighty-five Israelis and 900 Palestinians had lost their lives.

On August 29, 1993, Israel and the PLO agreed in the Oslo Accords to a timetable for Palestinian self-rule. The document, signed in September, called for limited autonomy of parts of Gaza and Jericho in the West Bank, with some vague promises of self-government after five years. Israel intended this agreement to function as a civilian arm of the Israeli military occupation forces, essentially making the PLO Israel's enforcer in the occupied territories. General Keith Dayton served five years as the US Security Coordinator for Israel and the PA. His leadership role included overseeing the training of PA forces. While the now-retired Dayton was a senior three-star officer, he never reported through a military chain of command. Rather, he reported directly to the Secretary of State, first Condoleezza Rice, under Bush, and later to Hillary Clinton, under Barak Obama. There were any number of reasons for this, not the least of which was that his mission was controversial among senior Pentagon officers, who argued that a US training mission, whose goal was to create a miliary force that cooperated with Israel, would raise serious objections among Arabs. As a US Army colonel said in 2009, "This is just a stupid idea. It makes us look like we're an extension of the Israeli occupation." This, of course, was the view that many Palestinians, including Hamas, also took.

According to Dr. Israel Shahak, chairman of the Israeli League of Human and Civil Rights, "The deeper intention of the Oslo Accord was to create an apartheid system." He questioned why Arafat ever signed a document that resulted in the permanent imposition of a Bantustan upon his people. As early as the 1990s, Palestinians were disillusioned with Arafat's one man, one-rule policies. His leadership was corrupt and ineffective, and the people demanded a change. Unwilling to give up control, Arafat signed the Oslo Accords, essentially duping the people into believing that they would realize their dream of a Palestinian state.

On September 1, 2000, accompanied by 1,000 Israeli soldiers, Ariel Sharon, Israel's prime minister, visited the Haram al Sharif Mosque, Islam's third-holiest site. As non-Muslims are forbidden entry, Palestinians viewed this as a deliberate desecration of their sacred site. In the ensuing riot, several Palestinians were killed, setting off the Second Intifada. During this period, Hamas, Islamic Jihad and al Aqsa Martyrs Brigade resorted to escalating numbers of suicide bombers. Up through August 2005, there had been sixty-eight suicide bombings, killing 587 Israelis. In addition, 500 soldiers and settlers were killed. Some 4,000 Palestinians lost their lives during the Second Intifada. In August 2004, the new head of Hamas in Gaza, Abdul Aziz al Rantissi, was killed in a targeted Israeli air strike. Hamas' founder, Sheikh Ahmad Yassin was assassinated in March 2004.

After Arafat's death in November 2004, Mahmoud Abbas was elected the PA's president and Hamas and Islamic Jihad agreed to suspend attacks on Israel to give Abbas time to secure international guarantees for a comprehensive ceasefire that would end more than four years of Intifada.

But then in August 2005, Prime Minister Ariel Sharon carried out what he called a "unilateral disengagement" from the Gaza Strip (unilateral means that he acted without prior consultation with the PA), pulling out 7, 800 Israeli settlers who had occupied the Gaza Strip for thirty-eight years. They comprised one-half of 1 percent of the population in Gaza, yet they occupied 20 percent of the land. An additional 10 percent of the Strip was under Israeli military control.

The Palestinian economy had for the most part been agricultural. After their lands were confiscated and their orchards uprooted to make way for Israeli settlements, Palestinians were obliged to become day laborers inside Israel. When former Prime Ministers Barak and Sharon closed off Gaza and the West Bank from Israel for long periods of time, denying Palestinians the right to enter, Palestinians suddenly found themselves without work and without money, unable to feed their families. According to the World Bank, 86 percent of Gazan households depend on food from the U.N. or other humanitarian agencies.

During Israel's thirty-eight-year occupation of Gaza, Palestinians we not allowed to build a seaport along the Mediterranean to export their goods. Similarly, they were forbidden to reconstruct an old, abandoned airport. Unless the Israeli government reversed their decisions, Palestinians would remain without a seaport or airport. Since the only way in and out of Gaza into Israel was through the Eretz checkpoint manned by Israeli soldiers, Israel was still able to cut off the supply of food and medicine, raw materials, water, fuel, gas and electricity at will. Gazans were still feeling the effects of previous Israeli attacks on their electricity plant. A year later some 50,000 people were still without power, and Netanyahu proposed cutting water and electricity to all of Gaza.

After the Israeli withdrawal the PA had plans to revitalize the Palestinian economy in the Gaza Strip, where unemployment had reached almost 90 percent in some areas, by encouraging investment and creating jobs. To accomplish this, Israel's cooperation was needed. However, almost two years later, with Gaza surrounded by concrete walls and high fencing, Israel still strictly controlled all access in and out of the Strip, including the Rafah Crossing between Gaza and Egypt, for both people and goods. With absolute control still firmly in the hands of the Israelis, the Gaza Strip was still cut off from the West Bank and from the rest of the world.

James D. Wolfensohn was President of the World Bank from 1995 to 2005 before becoming Middle East Envoy for the Quartet (the US, Russia, the EU and the U.N) in May 2005. He was tasked with monitoring the Israeli disengagement from Gaza and helping to heal the ailing Palestinian economy. He successfully raised nine billion dollars toward that effort. In November 2005, three months after Israel withdrew its settlers, he acted as mediator between Israel and the PA in the negotiation of transit routes for goods to and form Gaza. He also donated money of his own to help the Palestinians buy Israeli-owned greenhouses in Gaza, left there by the settlers. Both the US administration interference and the rise of Hamas to power and the subsequent boycott by Israel combined to derail his mission. A frustrated Wolfensohn returned to the US in April 2006.

On January 26, 2006, Hamas stunned the world by winning the long anticipated Palestinian election. President George Bush failed to understand that Hamas won because of allegations that the PA was corrupt and plagued with nepotism. Hamas won seventy-six out of the 132 seats in the Palestinian Parliament. The first thing Hamas did when it won the election was to offer Israel a long-term truce. The offer was ignored by both Israel and the US. Reprisal for voting the wrong way quickly followed both from the US and Israel in the form of sanctions on the part of the US while Israel cut off the Gaza Strip from the rest of the world, creating an open-air prison for what was then one million seven hundred thousand inmates, 55 percent of whom were under the age of eighteen.

It was not until July 2007 when Hamas took control of Gaza that Wolfensohn felt compelled to speak on record:

"Part of the reason the slide into violence happened, in my view, was that the conditions in Gaza deteriorated so terribly. If you recall, in the time of the withdrawal in 2005 there was a day or two when people looted but within forty-eight hours it was under control. Things were peaceful in Gaza, and this was not here because of an Israeli military presence. It was because the Palestinians recognized that if they wanted to have any hope, they needed to be in a more peaceful mode. I remember seeing the greenhouses while touring Gaza with Abbas and looking at the fruits and vegetables. It was a joyous atmosphere. 'Boy, we're about to get this going and we're going to have hotels by the beaches and we're going to have tourism and it's going to be fantastic, and the Palestinians really know how to be hosts.' But in the months after, when Sharon fell ill and Olmert took over, there was a clear change in attitude.

"At the same time powerful forces in the US administration worked behind my back. They did not believe in the border terminals agreement between Gaza and the West Bank and wanted to undermine my status as the Quartet emissary. The official who tore apart every aspect of the terminal agreement was Elliot Abrams, the neoconservative who was appointed deputy national security advisor in charge of disseminating democracy in the Middle East. (This information was made known in Haaretz on July 19, 2007, in an article by Shara Smooha entitled "All the Dreams We Had Are Now Gone.")

Palestinians still needed permits to travel within the occupied West Bank, between the West Bank and Gaza, and into Israel. Palestinians living in Gaza needed Israeli permission to leave Gaza at the Rafah Crossing which exits into Egypt. During the month of May 2007, the crossing was open four days. In July 2007 an estimated five thousand people were waiting to cross on either side of the Rafah Crossing.

On May 16, 2007, Israel renewed air strikes on the Strip, firing on a Hamas Executive Support Forces base in southern Gaza. Over the next two days, according to the Palestinian Center for Human Rights (PCHR) Israel intensified air attacks targeting civilian facilities. Israel said these attacks came in response to the launching of homemade rockets at Sderot, an Israeli border town in the Negev, in what was formally the Palestinian village of Najd. During this period Palestinian fighters did, in fact, continue to launch Kassam rockets into Sderot, killing two and injuring several others, bringing the number of Israeli deaths to nine since 2001.

According to PCHR, a May 20 Israeli air strike on the home of a Hamas politician killed seven members of his family and three other civilians. This response came during a week of fighting between Palestinian groups that claimed about fifty lives and news that the Bush administration intended to increase its funding and arming of the forces loyal to Mohammad Dahlan, President Abbas's security chief in the Gaza Strip, as part of a plan developed by Elliot Abrams to violently overthrow the democratically elected Hamas government. According to European observers, the US was grooming Dahlan to assume the presidency and restore Fatah to power. However, many in Fatah were uncomfortable with Dahlan's and Abbas's cooperation with the US and Israel and advocated for cooperation between Fatah and Hamas.

The main cause of tension in Gaza was over who controlled the Palestinian security services and how efficient these services were. Additional factors complicated matters. A multitude of armed rogue splinter groups had emerged since June 2006, making violence almost impossible to contain. Israel, in its effort to destroy Hamas, had separated Gaza from the West Bank and had isolated it almost completely from the world. Islamic Jihad, which refused to abide by Hamas's ceasefire with Israel, continued to fire Kassam rockets into Sderot.

After his election in January 2006, Hamas leader Ismail Haniyeh maintained his ceasefire pledge with Israel. In May 2007 he offered a ten-year truce with Israel in exchange for Israel's agreement to end the siege of Gaza and the West Bank. Israel did not respond to his offer. Violence erupted in Gaza on June 14 between Hamas and Fatah when Hamas forcibly removed Mohammad Dahlan's security forces from Gaza. Abbas then dismissed the government and declared the formation of an emergency government, thereby bringing an end to what remained of Palestinian unity.

With Hamas in control of Gaza, both the US and Israeli governments pledged their support to Abbas's Fatah, which was what they wanted all along. As a gesture of goodwill, Israel planned to ease roadblocks and security restrictions and release approximately eighty million dollars of the funds it had withheld from the PA in January 2006 when Hamas won the elections. In the interim, hundreds of thousands of workers had gone without a paycheck for one and a half years. The plan all along was to isolate Gaza and on July 16, 2007, the US forbid both Western Union and DHL from transferring money into the Gaza Strip.

According to US Secretary of State Envoy to the Middle East, David Welch, "We are supporting the legitimate security forces and enhancing them in order to establish a Palestinian entity which will be able to provide security and stability for Palestinians citizens, and we will be committed to this in the future." In a leaked report in June 2007, retired U.N. Special Envoy to the Middle East, Alvaro De Soto contradicted Mr. Welch's statement, saying, "The Americans clearly encouraged a confrontation between Fatah and Hamas and worked to isolate and damage Hamas and build up Fatah with recognition and weaponry."

In the meantime, the war between Hezbollah and Israel in Lebanon had just ended but a political crisis between Sunnis and Shiites continued with an intense three-week battle between Fatah al Islam and the Lebanese army inside a Palestinian camp in northern

Lebanon. This involved Elliot Abrams again. His idea was to covertly fund the Sunni-al Qaeda-like Fatah al Islam as a counterweight to Hezbollah. If any of this sounds familiar, it is because the CIA recruited and trained al Qaeda insurgents as a counterweight to the Russian army in Afghanistan in the late 70s. The irony here is that Israel did the same thing. It encouraged the rise of Hamas as a counterweight to the PA.

When Hamas won the election, the position of Prime Minister did not exist under the original constitution of the PA but was added in March 2003 at the insistence of the US which wanted a counterweight to Arafat. As a result, while the election allowed Abbas to retain the presidency, he was forced to share power with Ismail Haniyeh, the Hamas Prime Minister. However, the US imposed financial sanctions on Hamas and isolated it politically. Instead of helping Fatah through the transition and facilitating Palestinian unity and taking advantage of a real chance to include Hamas, the international community, and the US, in particular, pursued an aggressive policy of internal division thereby establishing the conditions for havoc in Gaza. As of July 14, 2007, Israel still maintained a complete ban on aid or have any contact with the Gaza Strip until Hamas recognized Israel's right to exist, a condition neither Jordan nor Egypt had to agree to in advance of negotiations.

Fast forward to 2024. Palestinians continue to live in what could only be described as Bantustans in the West Bank, and a concentration camp in Gaza, with Palestinians in East Jerusalem and the West Bank living under brutal apartheid management structures, as confirmed by B'Tselem, Israel's leading human rights organization.

In June 2024, the Israeli military handed over significant legal powers in the occupied West Bank to pro-settler civil servants working for Finance Minister Smotrich, in a move that will help accelerate Israel's illegal annexation of the West Bank. Michael Sfard, an Israeli human rights lawyer, said, "The bottom line is that for anyone who thought the question of annexation was foggy, this order should end any doubts because it transfers vast areas of administrative power from the military commander to Israeli civilians. This transfer will allow Smotrich and his appointees from his religious settler movement to further expand. It is currently home to millions of indigenous Palestinian Christians and Muslims. If Smotrich has his way these residents will be ethnically cleansed to clear the way for more settlers.

October 7 did not happen in a vacuum. It was the result of decades of brutal Israeli violence and the Palestinian effort to liberate itself from its stranglehold.

Do we condemn Hamas, or do we condemn an occupying power that makes armed struggle necessary for survival?

Agree with them or not, Hamas has taken up the mantle of resistance. The years of struggle they have waged and endured and continue to endure have made more of a material impact than any of us in the West could have imagined. Israel's government has said it is committed to the destruction of Hamas, but Hamas is an ideology, a steadfast liberation movement that cannot be defeated. Hamas has awakened the world to the plight of

the Palestinian people, and the students have have helped
by putting their struggles on the international stage. The
world will never be the same again.

Cast of Characters,
Events and Places

GOLAN HEIGHTS

The Golan is a region in southwestern Syria occupied by
Israel since 1967. Prior to1967, the Golan was home to
some 100,000 Syrians. The international community, with
the exception of Israel and the US, consider the Golan
Heights to be Syrian territory held by Israel under military
occupation. In November 2006, Syria's president Bashar
al Assad offered to make peace with Israel in exchange for
the return of the Golan Heights. Israel refused. In 2019,
President Trump broke with other powers by recognizing
Israel rule as sovereign on the Golan Heights, which it
annexed in 1981 in a move not recognized internationally.

LEBANON

The name of this country is derived from the Semitic root
LBN, which is linked to the world white, a reference, no
doubt, to the snow-covered Mount Lebanon.

THE LEVANT

Lebanon and Syria are called the Levant states. The term *Levant* derives from the Middle French word *levant,* the participle of *lever,* "to rise," as in *soleil levant,* "sun rising." Levant equates to the Arabic word *Mashriq,* "the land of the rising sun."

NORTHERN ISRAEL

The mountainous Galilee Region dominates northern Israel, extending twenty-five miles from the Mediterranean to the Sea of Galilee, also called Lake Tiberias. Its major cities include Tiberias, Haifa, Acre, Nazareth and Ein Hod. There are approximately seven million people living in Israel. Of that total, 75 percent are Jews and 20 percent are Palestinians or Arab Israelis, designated as such by the Israeli government. Of the more than two million people living in northern Israel, close to a million are Palestinian. Along the border with Lebanon, 650 feet away, there are some sixty thousand Israeli settlers who have had to flee their homes as a result of recent Hezbollah attacks. Israel is demanding Hezbollah pull its forces from the Lebanese-Israel border to the other side of the Litani River so these Israelis can return to their homes.

SOUTH LEBANON AND ITS PEOPLE

This is a region extending from the Awali River in the uppermost part of South Lebanon to Ras al Nakoura in the south, a distance of some fifty kilometers, and from the Mediterranean Sea in the west to the Syrian-Lebanese border in the Northeast. Some of the south's best-known towns include Jezzine, Sidon, Tyre, Nabatieh, Marjeyoun, Bint Jbeil and Nakoura on the Israeli border. Sixty percent of South Lebanon's residents are Shiites; the rest are

Christians. During the Israeli-Hezbollah war in 2006, some 800,000 residents from South Lebanon were forced to flee their homes.

THE ISRAELI OCCUPATION OF PALESTINIAN LAND

Since 1967, Israel has illegally occupied East Jerusalem, the West Bank, the Gaza Strip and the Golan Heights in Syria. It has extensive Israeli settlements in Jerusalem, the West Bank and the Golan. In 2005, it pulled its Jewish settlers out of the Gaza Strip.

PRE-1967 BORDER (ALSO CALLED THE GREEN LINE OR THE 1949 ARMISTICE LINE)

After the cessation of hostilities between the Arab countries and Israel in 1948, an armistice agreement was signed in 1949. The agreement delineated the borders of each party and designated a no man's land between them according to the location of the respective armies. This line demarcated the border between Israel and the West Bank and the Gaza Strip as recognized by the international community even though Israel did not specify, nor has it ever specified, the specific boundaries of its state. Although the line became known as the Green Line or, more commonly, the pre-'67 border, its proper name is the 1949 Armistice Line.

During the June 1967 Arab Israeli War, Israel crossed the Green Line to occupy the West Bank, the Gaza Strip and the Sinai, East Jerusalem and the Golan Heights. U.N. Resolution 242, adopted in November 1967 called for the withdrawal of Israeli forces from territories occupied during the 1967 war in return for an Arab pledge of full peace and recognition.

Egypt signed a peace treaty with Israel. In June, 1978, Sadat recognized Israel's right to exist and offered full peace.

In June 2007, Hamas recognized Israel's right to exist "on the pre-'67 border. The initiative even agreed to minor border justifications that could include some of the Israeli settlements illegally built in East Jerusalem. The Geneva Initiative, proposed by a group of distinguished Israelis and Palestinians suggested similar conditions in October 2003 in return for Israel's withdrawal of the Occupied West Bank. Israel never responded to either of these initiatives.

BALFOUR DECLARATION

The Balfour Declaration was issued on November 2, 1917. It read: His majesty's government views with favor the establishment in Palestine of a national homeland for the Jewish people and will use their best endeavors to facilitate the achievement of the object, it being clearly understood that nothing shall be done which may prejudice the civil and religious rights of existing non-Jewish communities in Palestine or the rights and political status enjoyed by Jews in any other country.

As Chaim Weizman said, in relation to Palestine, when he addressed the 1914 World Zionist Congress in Paris, "a land without people for a people without land," even though 700,000 Arabs lived there at the time. The pledge is generally viewed as one of the main catalysts of the Nakba, the ethnic cleansing of Palestine in 1948, and the conflict that ensued with the establishment of the State of Israel. The statement came in the form of a letter from Britain's then-foreign secretary, Arthur Balfour, addressed to Lionel Walter Rothschild, a figurehead of the British Jewish community.

SYKES-PICOT AGREEMENT

Under this 1916 agreement, the Ottoman provinces were divided into areas of British and French control, with Britain taking Palestine and Iraq. Britain's Mandate made it easy to establish self rule for the Jews at the expense of the Palestine Arabs who made up 90 percent of the population. The document was controversial because Britian had already promised the Arabs independence from the Ottoman Empire in the 1915 Hussein-McMahon correspondence. In the Sykes-Picot agreement, the British promised the French that the majority of Palestine would be under international administration, while the rest of the region would be split between the two colonial powers. In a meeting with Zionist leader Chaim Weizmann in 1922, Arthur Balfour and then-Prime Minister David Lloyd George reportedly said the Balfour Declaration "always meant an eventual Jewish state."

DAVID BEN GURION

Israeli's first Prime Minister. He had a lot to say about the Balfour Declaration. "If I were an Arab leader, I would never sign an agreement with Israel. It is normal; we have taken their country. It is true God promised it to us, but how could that interest them? Our God is not theirs. There has been Antisemitism, the Nazis, Hitler, Auschwitz, but was that their fault? They see but one thing: we have come, and we have stolen their country. Why would they accept that. (Quoted by Nahum Goldmann in Le Paraddoxe Juif)

"Let us now ignore the truth among ourselves. Politically we are the aggressors, and they defend themselves. The country is theirs, because they inhabit it, whereas we want to come here and settle down, and in their view, we want to

119

take away from them their country. Behind the terrorism (by the Arabs) is a movement, which though primitive, is not devoid of idealism and self-sacrifice." Ben Gurion quote on p. 91 of Chomsky's *Fateful Triangle*. The same quote also appears in Simha Flapan's *Zionism and the Palestinians*, p.141.)

"What is to be done with the Palestinian population," Military commander and politician Yigal Allon asked. Ben Gurion waved his hand in a gesture which said, "Drive them out." (Yitzhak Rabin's memoir, published in the *New York Times, October 123, 1979).*

HEZBOLLAH
Hezbollah, meaning Party of God, is a political and military party officially begun in 1985 as a local resistance movement against the 18-year-long illegal Israel occupation of South Lebanon. Ronald Regan first named such movements in the late '80s as "freedom fighters," a local population struggling to free itself from the yolk of a military occupation. The US and Israel, under George W. Bush and Ariel Sharon, and his successors, all call Hezbollah a terrorist organization while the Arab and Muslim world considers it a legitimate militant Shiite political party. Hezbollah receives financial support and weaponry from its mentor, Iran, the regional Shiite superpower. In June 2000 Israel withdrew from South Lebanon, ending its 18-year occupation. Hezbollah's successful guerrilla campaign is credited with achieving the withdrawal. Aside from its military wing, Hezbollah maintains a social service network which runs hospitals, free clinics and schools. After the Israeli-Hezbollah war ended in August 2006, the organization, with funds from

Iran, distributed $12,000 to each family whose houses were destroyed. The group, headed by Nasrallah since 1992, is one of the most influential political blocs in Lebanon and is often dubbed "a state within a state" due to its vast political and military networks. It is widely believed by analysts to be the only non-state actor in the region that can take on Israel. While Israel, the US and some western countries consider Hezbollah a terrorist organization, the EU classifies Hezbollah's military wing as a terrorist group but not its political wing.

HASSAN NASRALLAH

The spiritual and political leader of Hezbollah and one of the most powerful Arab Shia figures in the Middle East. He has been praised for driving Israel out of Lebanon but criticized for threatening Lebanese sovereignty because of close ties with Iran and Syria. Under his leadership, Hezbollah has grown from a local armed movement to the largest political party in Lebanon's recent history. In the 2018 parliamentary elections, it won more than 340,000 preferential votes, the most of any party in Lebanon since independence. In October 2021, Nasrallah said that Hezbollah had 100,000 fighters, making it the most powerful non-national armed organizations worldwide. To date, it is the only armed force to have forced Israel to retreat from an Arab country. Nasrallah has long been in Iran's Axis of Resistance, which includes Hezbollah, Hamas and Islamic Jihad and several Iraqi paramilitary groups. As of this writing, Hezbollah is listed as a terrorist organization by the US, UK, Germany, Australia, Canada, the Gulf's Cooperation Council and some in the Arab League, and its military wing by the EU. In contrast,

China and Russia among others, take a neutral stance or maintain some form of contract.

In 1982, Hezbollah launched a guerrilla campaign to drive Israel from Lebanon. Aside from attacking Israeli troops and outposts, Hezbollah also staged suicide bombings, including one against an Israeli military HQ in Tyre in November 1982 that killed at least seventy-five Israelis and upward of twenty Palestinians and Lebanese prisoners. Further attacks followed. They included the bombing of the US Embassy in Lebanon in April 1983, which killed at least seventeen Americans and more than thirty Lebanese. Hezbollah is blamed for the October 1983 attack on the US Marines barracks and French paratrooper outpost in Beirut, which killed 300, but has denied involvement.

Its political wing has become one of the most powerful parties in modern political Islam, with allies in Syria, Yemen, Iran and Palestine. In May 2000 Israel unilaterally withdrew from south Lebanon, the first time it had ended the occupation of an Arab territory without a treaty or security arrangement. The move validated Nasrallah's long-standing argument that only armed resistance can recover Arab land. In 2006, Israel launched an incursion into Lebanon after Hezbollah captured two Israeli soldier in a cross-border attack. Hezbollah said the kidnappings were to gain leverage for the release of Lebanese prisoners in Israel. Ariel Sharon had used the same tactic multiple times so a precedent had been set. Hezbollah claimed that if it had known Israel would launch such a massive attack on Lebanon, they would never have kidnapped the soldiers. Under Nasrallah's leadership of Hezbollah, modern Lebanon has been able to militarily defend itself against Israel, not least in the south. Its political wing has become one of the most powerful parties in modern political Islam, with allies in Syria, Iraq, Yemen and Palestine.

YAHYA SINWAR (HAMAS'S LEADER AND MILITARY STRATEGIST)

Sinwar, the leader of Hamas in the Gaza Strip, is believed to have masterminded the unprecedented Hamas attack that changed the course of Israeli-Palestinian history. He spent more than two decades behind bars in Israel, before being freed twelve years ago in a hostage deal his brother helped negotiate.

Born on October 29, 1962, he helped found the group's internal security apparatus in the late 1980s. He is called the butcher of Khan Younis for his role in rooting out suspected Palestinian informants for Israel and was imprisoned in Israel on four life sentences for killing Israeli soldiers and Palestinian collaborators. In 2006, Israeli soldier Gilad Shalit was captured by Hamas and held hostage in Gaza for five years. The man who guarded the captive solder was Sinwar's brother Mohammed. In 2011, Hamas freed the soldier in exchange for more than 1,000 Palestinian prisoners. Sinwar's was one of them. On October 7, Sinwar outsmarted Israel with the same hostage-taking tactic, resulting in Israel's deadliest day on record. The attack earned him widespread support among Palestinians, many of whom regard October 7 the result of decades of Israeli subjugation. His VIP status in prison and his return to Gaza where he still lives with the released prisoners helped Sinwar rise in the ranks to lead Hamas in Gaza.

BENJAMIN NETANYAHU

Netanyahu has held office six times, more than any other prime minister in the country's history. Re-elected in November 2022, leading the most right-wing coalition in Israel's history, the seventy-three-year-old Netanyahu promised to govern for all Israelis, regardless of political differences. Instead, his planned reforms have met with mass protests on a scale barely seen since the creation of Israel seventy-five years ago. He is facing one of the biggest crises in his long political life, amid the uproar over his government's attempts to change the way the country's judicial system works. His unrivaled success owes much to the image he has cultivated as the person who can best keep Israel safe from hostile forces in the Middle East. October 7 dramatically tarnished his image. Also, hanging over his political achievements and massive miscalculations, is the cloud of an ongoing criminal trial for alleged bribery, fraud and breach of trust, charges he fiercely denies. As a man described by The Times of Israel as "ultra divisive," his opponents see him as a danger to Israel.

About the Author

Cathy Sultan is an award-winning author of three nonfiction books: *A Beirut Heart: One Woman's War; Israeli and Palestinian Voices: A Dialogue with Both Sides and Tragedy in South Lebanon. The Syrian,* a political thriller, was her first work of fiction, followed by *Damascus Street, An Ambassador to Syria. Omar's Choice is the* fourth of a quartet on the Syrian conflict. Sultan is also a peace activist who served on the Board of Directors of Interfaith Peace Builders (now Eyewitness Palestine) She took her first trip to Israel-Palestine in March 2002 and subsequently co-led five delegations to Israel/Palestine, including a trip to Gaza in 2012.

Sultan won USA's Best Book of the Year Award in 2006 for her memoir *A Beirut Heart;* USA's Best Book of the Year Award in 2006 in the category of History/ Politics for *Israeli and Palestinian Voices. Tragedy in South Lebanon* was nominated for Best Book of the Year in the Category of Political Science in 2008; *Damascus Street* was a finalist for both the Eric Hoffer Award and the Montaigne Medal Award and *An Ambassador to Syria* won the Independent Press Award for Historical Fiction in 2022.

www.ingramcontent.com/pod-product-compliance
Lightning Source LLC
Chambersburg PA
CBHW030942090426
42737CB00007B/507